MORE I Learned About Flying from That

Also from the Editors of *Flying*

I Learned About Flying from That

More I Learned About Flying from That

by the Editors of *Flying*

Compiled by Nigel Moll, Associate Editor

AN ELEANOR FRIEDE BOOK

Macmillan Publishing Company
New York

Collier Macmillan Publishers
London

Macmillan Publishing Company
866 Third Avenue, New York, N.Y. 10022
Collier Macmillan Canada, Inc.

Library of Congress Cataloging in Publication Data
Main entry under title:
More I learned about flying from that.
"An Eleanor Friede book".
A collection of articles which appeared previously in
Flying.
1. Aeronautics. 2. Airplanes—Piloting. I. Moll,
Nigel. II. Flying (Chicago, Ill.)
TL553.M83 1984 629.132'52 84-3906
ISBN 0-02-579350-0

10 9 8 7 6 5 4 3 2 1

Printed in the United States of America

Substantially all the material in this work was first published in *Flying* magazine.

Contents

Contributors

Preface

Pilots have always liked to hangar fly. For those unfamiliar with the term, it refers to the practice of huddling around a potbellied stove in the corner of a dark hangar on a stormy night, and telling about and listening to adventures. Unlike fish stories, though, hangar flying has its lessons, to be stored away for retrieval later in the cockpit.

And hangar flying doesn't have to be around the stove. *Flying* magazine's "I Learned About Flying from That" column started in May 1939 as a means of bringing, once a month, one pilot's misadventure to the attention of tens of thousands of others. The column serves as a confessional and as a way for pilots to learn from others' mistakes. It is this firsthand look at some of aviation's trickier moments that makes the column so popular and valuable. And if a pilot, by confessing, however crass his mistake, can prevent a recurrence with another pilot, he feels better about his error. It becomes a more worthwhile episode when others can benefit.

This book is a collection of some of the best "ILAFFTs" to have been published in *Flying* since the release of the first collection in 1976 in a book entitled *I Learned About Flying from That*. This new edition, *MORE I Learned About Flying from*

That, focuses primarily on incidents relevant to today's flying. Pilots still have to deal with the vagaries of weather, human judgment, and even mechanical malfunction, but fewer are getting hopelessly lost in our modern environment of electronic navaids. Nearly all the incidents took place in the past seven years, and they involve today's airplanes and pilots. We hope that makes the lessons doubly valuable.

Nigel Moll
Associate Editor, *Flying*

More Than a Little Luck

Whether they care to admit it or not, pilots do not survive through skill alone. Although skill is far and away the primary ingredient in safe flying, luck plays a definite role. This role is more apparent on some flights than on others, and it's the luck-laden ones that tend to bring a tingle to the back of the neck years later. In such a rigid activity as flying, with all its precise procedures based on scientific principle and common sense, luck would seem to have no place. Like it or not, though, it's there. The more experienced the pilot, the less likely is he to admit that Lady Luck played a part in the successful outcome of a potential mishap. Beginners, however, led on by the torch of optimism and blinkered by blissful unawareness, tend to be more willing to hold luck responsible for much of their success.

Sometimes a pilot will get in far enough above his head that luck is about the only card left to play. That overextension of abilities might not be the pilot's doing either, as becomes apparent in two of the four episodes recounted in the chapter that follows. Leaving skill out of the equation for a moment, a midair collision has to be one of the largest doses of bad luck dispensed to pilots. The scan for traffic is, of course, the antidote, but there's no denying the misfortune that brings together two airplanes that, fractions of a second sooner or later, would have passed safely if uncomfortably.

Luck can be the savior in situations that have been brought about by a series of judgment errors that began early in the game. While the wise pilot makes every effort to conduct each flight so precisely that there is no room for luck—bad luck, anyway—to play a part, the best-laid plans sometimes go awry, as you shall see. . . .

Because of heavy air traffic in the Chicago terminal control area, departure control kept us down low at 2,500 feet and ran us out over the lake before we could make a turn to the south toward our destination and resume the climb to 15,000. As we approached the shoreline of Lake Michigan, we entered the clouds and lost outside visual reference. Bob was flying and I was working the radios and keeping our flight log. The air was smooth as our Merlin IIB's twin jetprop engines propelled us along with authority. In our airplane, with all the amenities of most airliners plus better pressurization, I could easily imagine myself in the front office of a much larger, grander aircraft. Our Merlin emitted a certain aura of perfect safety, of absolute security.

In the middle of a logbook entry I looked up, trying to scan the horizon beyond our windshield. All I saw, of course, was a bright whitish gray void of indeterminate depth. Bob had watched me do this many other times when we'd been flying in the soup. In my several years of flying, I've made a conscious effort to keep a sharp watch for other traffic. Some pilots I've flown with have considered me almost paranoid. My rebuttal has always been the old axiom, "Better a stiff neck than a broken one."

Now, in our Merlin's cockpit, the pilot could no longer contain himself. "Carl, you're not going to see anything out there. This stuff's so thick even our wingtips look a little bit fuzzy."

"I know," I said, "but looking's a habit with me." And yet I did not agree completely that it was useless to look. What of those times when you break into clear air, sometimes between layers of clouds, and it's not obvious you've done so if you're being overly attentive to your flight instruments? Also, there's always the chance another airplane could be nearby—maybe some VFR pilot who's lost. Or another IFR carrying a load of ice and losing altitude. Or an aircraft in an emergency descent after an explosive decompression. Anything *is* possible. Besides, I feel my habit of doing a lot of looking enhances my safety and that of the people who share the sky with me; admittedly, this is true mainly in VFR conditions.

Several seconds later, still occupied with the flight log, I glanced up again and saw *another airplane*! Less than a thousand feet away, in a head-on collision course with us, was a twin, quite clearly a Cessna 320. In these microseconds the dimensions of time changed. My realization of our situation and our subsequent actions took only fractions of seconds.

I grasped the control yoke in my right hand and called loudly to Bob while pointing my left index finger. There was just enough time, I judged, that if I banked the airplane while Bob was flying it and he instinctively fought against my control inputs, I could still maneuver the Merlin to avoid collision. And I would have acted if he hadn't just when he did.

Bob turned left with a hard, fast roll to a bank attitude of about 50 degrees. The Cessna was slightly right of head-on, where it would have hit our right wing. Regardless of the regulations, left was the way to go; right and we wouldn't have made it. Regulations are fine when you've got lots of time, but when it's close, you have to do whatever works. The Cessna flashed past within 50 to 100 feet of us.

Now Bob rolled back to level flight. We looked at each other, then back through the open door to the cabin at our passengers. They were—unbelievably—engrossed in conversation and oblivious to our stares. I think we'd expected to see white faces as a result of our nearly aerobatic maneuver; but no, they appeared totally at ease and unaware of anything out of the ordinary. You might deduce from this that we routinely flew like barnstormers and that our people were accustomed to it. The truth is that Bob's maneuver, though fast, had been smooth and coordinated. Or maybe they thought we'd hit one of those legendary "air pockets."

Next, Bob picked up his mike and told ATC we'd just deviated from our assigned heading to avoid another aircraft, head-on at our altitude. ATC responded that they had no such traffic on radar and definitely not under IFR control. If you've flown much in a radar environment you know that equipment does not see all traffic and the controllers may not always report all that radar does detect. It's always good, therefore, to keep your eyes open.

I'm fairly certain the pilot who almost killed the five of us, himself or herself, and any innocent victims riding in that Cessna 320 had intentionally flown illegal IFR. Perhaps he thought IFR flights always flew right *at* thousand-foot levels. I wonder if he knew that one of Chicago's skyscrapers, which was ahead and not too far left of his course, was only 100 feet below him.

I didn't hear of any crashes that day so I imagine he made it down safely somewhere. As for me, I'll continue my habit of doing a lot of looking—for the innocent majority and the guilty few.

Luck played a large part in keeping these two airplanes apart, without doubt; but the copilot's habit (a strange habit, some might say) of looking outside for traffic even while in the soup was what finally saved the day.

In the next incident, two pilots (one below in a high-winger, the other above in a low-winger) were unfortunate enough to meet aloft. Luck, however, brought the airplanes together in such a fashion that they both remained flyable (barely) after the impact.

Early in the afternoon on one of those golden, clear fall days in the Washington, D.C., area, I had an after-lunch instrument student. With my student in the seat, under the hood, we made an instrument takeoff. We were flying out of Hyde Field, Maryland, about five miles south of Andrews Air Force Base. The sky for miles around was as clear of aircraft as it was of clouds; nevertheless, my head was on a swivel. We climbed slowly to 1,400 feet, below the Washington TCA.

Suddenly, without warning, we were jarred out of our comfort by a loud, soul-shaking crash. Our aircraft was thrown violently downward and to the left of its flight path. For an instant, I felt numb and my perception and awareness went blank, but I was galvanized into action when I saw the shreds and chunks of my aircraft falling all around me. It was like a slow-motion replay: I was a spectator watching the pieces of the airplane slowly tumble and fall. My God! We'd had a midair collision. I felt, but wasn't sure, that the aircraft was in a diving spiral, heading for terra very firma at an alarming rate. I went for the throttle—a reflex reaction born of training and long experience—and I shoved it home. For what seemed an interminable amount of time, I held full right stick and rudder to get her straight and level.

"My God!" screamed my student. "Save us! Do something!"

"We aren't dead yet," I replied. Strangely enough, I felt myself growing calmer as he became more excited. I was going to exercise a lifetime of flying experience, and I knew I was going to save two lives in the process. Our salvation lay in the fact that, for the moment, at least, and with a lot of physical pressure, the horizon seemed to be in its proper place, the engine was roaring, and our rate of descent was zero. I was holding nearly full right rudder and aileron just as if I was in a twin with one engine windmilling.

Gently, I experimented with the controls I had remaining. Every time I let her go just the least bit from the aileron full-right position, that left wing felt as though it was going to barrel roll, with me in the barrel.

I never saw the other aircraft and it was still nowhere to be seen. I tried to assess the damage. My left wing was mostly gone, its ragged stub to within a few inches, it seemed, of the spar. Keeping that airplane in the air and landing it safely became the only things I wanted to do for the rest of my life. But to land I needed altitude control, and when I tried to reduce power and lift the nose, we'd approach the classic spin entry. Anywhere under 110–115 mph was *dangerous*.

I looked around. National Airport was ten miles to the left; Dulles about 20 miles farther left; Andrews AFB was eight miles to the right. Andrews looked bigger and right there, probably with a lot less traffic and with fire wagons and ambulances. Andrews became my target.

Radio. I had shouted at my student to call someone, but he froze on the mike. Would it work for me? 121.5. "Mayday, dammit, midair for Cessna 271, eight miles southwest. Emergency landing instructions—I hope." Those competent, godlike voices from the ground, if they heard me, sure would sound good right now—except that those voices couldn't help me make a left turn. We could drift to the right only, and at the sickening rate of about one degree per second. So, I planned my approach to the nearest—not necessarily active—7,500-foot runway so that I could stay to the left, needing only right turns or left skids to line up. "Cessna 271, radar contact, seven miles southwest, cleared for straight-in zero one right." Seven miles, about five more minutes, and all I had to do was pray that the remainder of the wing would stay with me and that I could hold altitude and make corrections with the three lifesaving S's: small, smooth, and slow. The emergency procedures I had learned flying B-17s in the air war in Europe were with me today when, after nearly thirty years of flying, I finally needed them.

We passed the outer marker—a welcome sound. I realized I was cramped and my ribs were hurting. I asked my student if he would tighten my seat belt. I'll be doggoned if he didn't loosen the belt completely, and it came all the way off. I darn near lost the machine at that point. Finally, he got the belt tightened around me again, and I was braced there like a stuffed porcupine.

As we neared the runway, I kept talking to myself. "For heaven's sake, don't bring the power back. Don't let the airspeed die out. Keep her moving. Get safely on the runway. Keep on flying. Fly it right down to the runway!"

Slowly, gently, slowly, the runway threshold drew closer. My student's tenseness seemed to choke him; he grabbed the handhold with both hands and was sitting bolt upright, staring unblinking straight ahead. Finally, over the fence with full power; level, skimming over that beautiful concrete with my wheels six inches absolute, I reduced the rpm by about 200 and both wheels kissed the runway. Then I chopped the power, slowed it with brakes, and turned off the active.

About ten seconds later we were surrounded by rotating red lights and what seemed like hundreds of people, all gazing in amazement at that five feet of wing that wasn't there. I jumped out and looked. The aileron was hanging on about one-quarter inch of residual hinge. Just one-quarter inch more gone and you would have read about this in the statistics. I turned, already trying to forget the missing wing section while I reveled in the joy of another pilot who survived. I was glad to be there with the crowd.

The following story appeared the next day in *The Washington Post*:

A German engineer who has had a pilot's license for only one month landed his single-engine airplane safely on one wheel yesterday after a midair collision with another light plane in Charles County, officials at a local airport reported.

Egon Rottman, in this country on an exchange program, landed his Cherokee Archer 180 on a foam-covered runway at Maryland Airport in Pomonkey, Maryland, after its left landing gear was knocked off in a collision with a Cessna 172 almost an hour earlier, according to Gilbert Bauserman, an owner of the airport.

Rottman "did a beautiful job landing" after the collision, Bauserman said. He said the collision occurred when the two pilots lost sight of each other for several seconds because the low-wing Cherokee, with a blind spot below the pilot, was flying above the high-wing Cessna, whose blind spot is above the pilot.

Rottman circled the airport for forty-five minutes after the crash, Bauserman said, in order to burn all the fuel from the tank on his plane's left side so that it would not explode and burn in case he crashed.

A local volunteer fire department covered 1,200 feet of the airport's runway with foam while Rottman circled the landing field, Bauserman said, and squirted foam on the plane as it landed.

Luck may have kept the writer's airplane airborne initially, but a large measure of skill was required to keep it flyable right down to the runway. In the next confessional, a fortunate lay of the land kept four pilots and one exotic airplane out of the treetops. As the situation became stickier, each front-seat pilot became less inclined to assume command. Good fortune, and some sweaty-palm piloting, rescued a planeload from the consequences of several dubious decisions.

I had always dreamed of flying an Aerostar. Slim-hipped and trim, it looks fast sitting still. When Frank, a former groundschool student of mine, wheeled up to the ramp in the latest model, I just couldn't stand it anymore.

"Frank," I said, "what a gorgeous airplane. I'll bet that sure would be a lot of fun to fly."

"John, get in and fly the thing."

"Oh, no," I protested, "I'm not about to fly that expensive piece of equipment without your being with me." (Mistake number one.)

"I'll go with you. Jump in." It was more than I needed. I clambered into the left front seat. Frank slid in front with me, while my wife Martha and my friend Bill buckled up in the rear. This gave us four pilots in one airplane—more than enough for plenty of trouble.

Just as I had dreamed, the performance was astounding. The rate of climb on this clear Alaskan day was 3,000 feet per minute. We charged across the countryside at speeds I had never seen before.

Eventually, I began to feel guilty at the thought of burning nearly 40 gph of someone else's fuel and reluctantly headed back to the airport. On the downwind leg I had my hands full getting this sleek beauty to slow down. We thundered along for miles while I struggled to get below gear-extension speed.

As I turned base, I realized that I had flown too far downwind and would have a long slow final. I felt I had to comment on my poor planning. What I meant to say was, "Boy, this is bad pilot technique. Here I am low and slow on final, dragging the airplane in with gear and flaps down." That's what I *meant* to say. However, what I *actually* said was, "Boy, I'd sure be in trouble if I lost an engine now." (Mistake number two.)

Frank, eager to show how well his beloved beauty could perform on one engine, said, "Oh, no, let me show you. I'll simulate zero thrust." Then he pulled the right throttle back to idle position.

I realized that the smart thing to do would be to continue to the airport and land. But that would deprive Frank of the pleasure of showing off his beloved beauty's single-engine performance. So I said, "I'll do a go-around." (Mistake number three.)

The threshold flashed by as I pushed the mixtures forward. Suddenly Martha said, "John, he *feathered* it!" I couldn't believe it! I looked over my shoulder at the right prop and sure enough, it was feathered. Now we really were in trouble. The best choice was still to land. But when I looked back at the airport I decided we didn't have enough room left to land without crashing into trees at the other end.

As I was getting the power in, Frank hollered, "I'll get the flaps," and I answered, "I'll get the gear."

At this point Frank leaned back in his seat with satisfaction and said, "Watch this baby climb now."

"Frank, it's not climbing, it's descending." It was obvious that if the trend continued, we would soon be in the trees.

"You didn't raise the gear."

"Yes, I did."

"No, you didn't. It's not up."

I looked at the gear lights. Frank was right. It wasn't up. The realization struck like a thunderbolt. In an Aerostar, the hydraulic pump for the gear and the flaps is on the right engine! What was worse, this one didn't have the optional electric backup pump. We weren't going to be able to get the gear and flaps up. This airplane was going nowhere but down.

I felt cheated. I would never have feathered an engine this close to the ground. But here I was with a planeload of people and an engine feathered at 100 feet! The only thing to do was to look for the best place to crash.

"Put it on the road."

"It's too crooked. It's your airplane. You take it."

"No, you take it. I'll try to get the engine started."

I was holding blueline, but it became obvious we weren't going to clear the next clump of trees. My plan was to flare at the top of the trees and reduce power on the good engine just before touching the treetops.

Miraculously, the airplane ballooned in the flare and we skimmed over the trees. That exposed a little valley and a small river wriggling its way to the ocean. As we followed the river downstream, I experimented with slower and slower airspeeds.

By the time we reached the ocean I had discovered that by flying at the edge of the stall buffet I could keep from descending and sometimes even eke out a 50-fpm climb. While we were circling over the ocean at 100 feet, Frank was finally able to restart the engine. Downwind again at the airport, I made a firm resolve that in future everyone would understand the rules before takeoff.

Frank, who didn't really understand what had just happened, broke the tense silence. "It should have climbed better than that. Let's try it again to see what the problem was."

If he did try it again, Frank probably did so alone. The next incident proves that perseverance is not always admirable in

flying: while landing in a gusty crosswind, this pilot's airplane suffered a prop strike. But he didn't know it and took off for the return leg. He wished he hadn't.

The wind over the valley was causing the airplane to bounce around like a Ping-Pong ball. Attempts at trimming were futile; just as I got everything balanced, the bottom would seem to fall out of the sky. For a fair-weather flier, I had my hands full. Except for some high, thready cirrus clouds, the sky was a clear, beautiful blue.

I was en route to Jasper, Tennessee, to practice some landings at a small airstrip there. Jasper is surrounded by scenic mountains, the airport is attractive, there is little traffic, and the people are friendly.

I was flying out of Chattanooga in a Grumman-American AA-1A Trainer. A slight crosswind had nudged me on takeoff at Chattanooga. I was uncomfortable with crosswinds, particularly on landings, but I thought I could handle them. After all, I had plenty of hours in the Trainer, and I had never gotten into trouble, no matter what the wind conditions were. But that little nudge, just as I lifted off, gave me a tiny chill of apprehension.

The closer I got to Jasper, the worse the bouncing became. It was like flying in a sky full of invisible potholes, and I seemed to lurch from one to another. I finally had the strip in sight and called up unicom.

As I looked down on the wind sock, the friendly, drawling voice on the radio confirmed what my eyes told me. There was a gusty, 90-degree crosswind on the strip—not auspicious conditions for someone who is uncomfortable with crosswinds to practice landings.

Unconsciously, I made my decision. I was at Jasper, and I was going to give it a shot. If things got too rough, I'd head back to Chattanooga. I went through the prelanding checklist and announced my downwind. Flaps were down, and I was throttling back and turning onto base when the Trainer seemed to get booted in the tail. The airplane lurched, then settled. I turned on final—and watched the runway drift way to the left of the windshield. I couldn't believe it. I had to wave off.

I pushed in the throttle and hit the flaps switch. As the flaps started coming up, I began a climb to pattern altitude. My hands had begun to sweat. This time I flew a wider pattern and set up a crab. I was going to make this landing. I went through the checklist again, announced downwind, and made my turn to base. Everything seemed to be all right. The airplane was still bouncing a bit, but the runway was right where I wanted it, and I relaxed. Then the drifting started again, and before I knew it, I was waving off another landing. I swore under my breath and started around again.

The wind just couldn't be that bad. I knew I could handle it, and I wanted to prove that I could. By the third wave-off, I was blindly determined to get on the ground.

I decided that the Trainer's wings, coupled with full flaps, gave the wind too big a target. This time, I'd go in with half flaps and keep some power on. I set the flaps and turned base. This time I was going to get my wheels on the ground.

Turning short final, the Trainer was still bucking and jerking. I had the left wing lowered into the wind and was driving for the deck. It was the best approach I'd made all day. Thinking that the problem must have been the flaps, I figured I had things whipped. It never occurred to me that the wind might have slackened. Just as I flared, the wind hit with a vengeance.

The right main gear hit first as the left wing came up. The Trainer's nose suddenly pitched down, and there was an indescribable noise, something like the sound of a lawn mower running over a metal pipe.

The nose was pitching up again, and I was correcting for all I was worth, trying to level the wings and get the airplane firmly on the ground. I pulled the power off, and we were down and rolling. The Grumman was still shuddering as the wind hit it and tried to force it off the runway.

As I hit alternate brakes in an attempt to taxi in a straight line, a delayed reaction set in and my legs began to shake. Reaching up, I unlatched the canopy and cracked it open. My face felt bathed in cold water as the perspiration dried. I resisted the urge to look back and see if I'd left pieces of the airplane on the runway; for an instant, I was afraid of what I might find.

As I taxied back for takeoff, I calmed down and took stock. Everything seemed to be okay. If the undercarriage was damaged, I hadn't noticed it while taxiing. All the instruments were in the green. The engine sounded okay. I stood on the brakes and ran the engine up higher than usual for the mag check, and nothing came apart. My pretakeoff checks complete, I watched the wind sock. When it sagged, I released the brakes and began my takeoff roll.

The Trainer weaved a bit on the runway, and the instant the wheels broke free, I was blown off the runway heading. I stayed low for a while to build airspeed, then climbed out and headed back to Chattanooga. All the way back, I kept reviewing what had happened.

I had proved that I could get the airplane on the ground in bad crosswinds and had come through it apparently unscathed. True, I left Jasper like a felon fleeing the scene of a crime, but no harm was done. Still, the rough air on the way back kept a nagging doubt alive: I should have shut down and checked the airplane over.

The landing in Chattanooga was a piece of cake. If there was a crosswind, I didn't notice it. I taxied to the ramp and shut down. Tying the Trainer down, I glanced at the landing gear. Just as I thought; everything was okay. Bless those sturdy little legs. As I walked away, I looked back and felt a rush of blood to my face.

The prop tips were curled! The cause of the noise in Jasper was suddenly clear. I'd hit the runway with more than the wheels. I instantly recalled a local flier of some fame who had taken off in a reworked Globe Swift. One prop blade was cracked at the hub under the spinner; while cruising along, he threw the blade. The unbalanced engine tore itself right out through the bottom of the cowling. The Swift went into a flat spin, and the pilot was killed in the crash.

I had been lucky and I knew it. I knew the capabilities of my aircraft; it was just my own capabilities that I had misjudged. Overconfidence in my flying ability, plus stupid pride and angry determination, almost put me in a permanent losing situation. I should have returned to Chattanooga when I saw that conditions were bad; failing that, I should at least have looked the airplane over after the hard landing.

I had been forgiven this time, but I might not be so lucky again. Overconfidence and anger make poor copilots.

Heavy Weather

Of all the variables under which a pilot operates, weather has to be the most challenging. While there are formulae for figuring out the effect of altitude on airspeed or the effect of baggage on the center of gravity, weather cannot be predicted so precisely or in such hard and fast ways. Weather has patterns, instead, and only the most naive pilot places absolute faith in weather forecasting—the dubious art of predicting the conditions that will result from certain patterns. Weather patterns can be learned, and sometimes flying is the best teacher of how weather systems work.

The question of getting weather experience is similar to that of the chicken and the egg: the rules ordain that "thou shalt not fly in weather unless instrument-rated and equipped." The idea, of course, is not to fly *in* weather until legally entitled to do so, and it is this limbo period between receiving the private license and moving on to the instrument rating that puts pilots at perhaps their greatest exposure to weather risk as they strive, at all costs, to fly around or under low clouds. Encounters with weather can scare the heck out of pilots new and old, as can be seen from the experiences recounted in this chapter.

We begin with a doctor and his wife, who jokingly used to label flights as one-Valium, two-Valium or three-Valium trips. After this trip, from Houston to San Antonio in their new Seneca equipped with everything but radar or Stormscope, they had to devise a new rating system—thanks to a thunderstorm that was shooting the same approach.

Houston FSS reported numerous thunderstorms west of San Antonio, Texas, which was 800 overcast and seven miles. By the time we had driven to the airport and packed the airplane, the weather update reported scattered thunderstorms, with San Antonio 1,000 overcast and seven miles. We climbed through 8,000 feet of cloud at Houston and rode in the sunshine at 12,000 feet all the way to San Antonio. As we began the descent through a valley in the clouds, we saw cloud-to-cloud lightning but the air was smooth. We entered solid cloud at 8,000 feet. As we were vectored in a large right-hand circle for the Runway 3R ILS, we had moderate turbulence and rain. Approach was working four other aircraft, and my careful monitoring of both sides of their transmissions gave no hints of the coming events.

Still in solid cloud, we descended to 3,000 feet, where we were given our last right turn onto the final approach course. As we banked, I looked down through a large hole and saw Kelly Air Force Base. It was at that precise moment I made my first goof: I said to myself, "All this cloud and rain, and we are going to break out at 3,000 and have a visual approach." Then I heard, "Seneca 63 Mike, fly heading 300 degrees, intercept the localizer at or above 2,100 feet, cleared for ILS 3R approach and, uh, 63 Mike, how much fuel do you have on board?" I promptly said I had 3-1/2 hours. Approach then told me to contact the tower. At that point, I committed the second goof, or lapse. Why had the controller interrupted his "cleared for approach" instructions to ask my fuel status when the time from the outer marker to the missed-approach point at 120 knots was only 2 minutes 20 seconds? I was about to ask when the altimeter neared 2,100 feet and the localizer needle began to center. I was busy with approach flaps and gear, and going through the prelanding checklist, when it happened.

Those who have been inside a thunderstorm know what "it" is, and those who haven't cannot believe how bad it can be. "It" refers to the blue green color followed by near blackness; the hail so loud that you cannot stand the noise; the thought that the windshield cannot stand up to the pounding, that it will disintegrate at any second; and the incredible turbulence. My left hand was thrown so violently that I could not depress the push-to-talk switch on the yoke. My right hand was unable to tune the tower frequency because I couldn't keep it near the radio; the upward leaps of the airplane forced my right hand down onto the throttle levers, reducing power. The upward flailings of my right hand increased the power and turned my audio-panel toggle switches on again. My head was hitting the top of the cockpit even with my belt tight and the seat in the lowest position. I remembered an accident report in which the pilot struck the ceiling so hard that he was seriously injured and subsequently lost control of the aircraft.

I was able to maintain a descent to 1,600 feet, keep the localizer needle reasonably centered, tune to tower frequency, report the outer marker and the weather, and turn on the panel lights. I continued to wrestle with the wildly active instruments.

A voice that was only slightly louder than the sound of the hail came through the speaker: "63 Mike, say altitude." My eyes were on the attitude gyro, but a quick glance at the altimeter showed 2,600 feet . . . 2,600 feet? How can I be flying at approach speed with gear and approach flaps down and manifold pressure at 16 inches, and still gain 1,000 feet in about 45 seconds? It's easy inside a thunderstorm, that's how. Having gained 1,000 feet inside the marker, still climbing and still worrying about the windshield, I declared a missed approach.

Someone who was obviously more comfortable and secure than we were then came on with the most complex holding instructions I've ever heard. With my arms and feet flying uncontrollably about the cockpit, my pencil now in the rear baggage area along with my lap pad, my head banging against the cabin ceiling, my approach plates somewhere under the seat, I managed to convey our predicament to the ground with something like, "Forget the holding, give me a vector out of this stuff." We got prompt vectors to VFR conditions and were offered another approach, a deal that I declined rather impolitely.

We flew at 2,000 to 2,400 feet on a southerly heading and broke out beneath an overcast. We were given vectors to Devine, Texas, which was the closest airport. Now we were home free, right? Don't count on it. Troubles seem to come in batches and our day wasn't over. I overflew the airport at Devine and established that there was a strong north wind. I flew a pattern for Runway 35. While we were turning base, the airport apparently received the first gust of another storm as the wind changed 180 degrees. We floated past the wind sock but we finally landed, using every inch of the 3,500-foot runway. How ironic to make it through a big storm and almost lose the airplane at the end of a runway on a downwind landing. Goof number three.

We had lost all the outside glass and there was a gouge in the fiberglass portion of the vertical stabilizer. There were also many small hail pings, but nothing to prevent flying. After thirty minutes we returned to San Antonio. The Piper distributor there, a friend of mine, saw us taxiing in; "You're really lucky you didn't arrive forty-five minutes ago," he said. "We've just had the worst storm I've ever seen." He's in his seventies. He said there had been several inches of hail on the airport, and even forty-five minutes later there was 8 to 10 inches of water on some of the taxiways.

The pilot learned that ceiling and visibility are not the only concerns inside the marker. He also won't pass off unusual questions from the controller.

Here's an episode that bred some respect for the apparently calm region ahead of a violent thunderstorm. The pilot thought he was in the clear, but he had another think coming.

It was a clear, warm night, and a sultry breeze played out of the south. Kansas City International shimmered twenty minutes to the north, only slightly removed from the sea of light that was the city. Out to the west, a cold front was having its own Fourth of July. Virile enough to struggle over the Canadian Rockies, gathering momentum as it slid down the back side, the front had come howling out of the Dakotas, licking the ground with tornadoes. I had seen many such fronts—summers in Kansas were like that.

"Lawrence 30, you're radar contact. Maintain 4,500, heading 340. Expect Runway 9."

"Okay, 4-point-5, 340, and Runway 9 for Lawrence 30. How far out is that weather?"

"It's painting at about 50 miles. We got a report they had to abandon the control tower when it went through Salina—high winds. This your last trip, 30?"

"Sure is. We canceled the 10:45. Figured the front would be here by then."

Five passengers boarded the old Cherokee Six in Kansas City, and the aft baggage area was full. I sighed with relief at how smoothly the turnaround had gone. At this time of night, folks were often late, irritable, and long since separated from their luggage. I had waited an extra fifteen minutes in the hope of snagging some people off the last flight and had gotten two. We were back in the air about 9:45. Southbound now, I watched the languid oasis of Lawrence growing in the windshield and marveled at how such calm could prevail with such fury nearby. There was not a ripple in the air.

"Approach, Lawrence 30, how far west have you got that weather now?"

"Thirty, it looks like about thirty miles."

The show was truly impressive. Continuous lightning backlit huge white thunderheads. Black rain shafts stood like a forest beneath. It was awesomely beautiful, commanding almost our full attention. I noticed a long, narrow cloud ahead that seemed scarcely 50 feet thick and oddly symmetrical. It crossed our flight path at an angle of perhaps 20 degrees and was slightly higher, looking for all the world as though someone had drawn a gracefully curving line in the night.

"Approach, Lawrence 30. Wonder if we could descend to 2-point-5. We'd like to duck under some cloud."

"Thirty, that's approved. At 2,500 you'll be clear of the TCA, squawk 1200, and you're cleared to change to advisory frequency. See you tomorrow night."

In ten minutes we'd be on the ground. Don, the other pilot on duty that night, and I would be heading home long before things got nasty.

The first bump, a pothole, hit short and hard just as we were slipping beneath the cloud. I rolled gently to the left in response. What happened next is a jumble of visual impressions and the acid recollection of sheer terror. I was sure we had midaired. Something I couldn't see rammed us in the belly as I rolled to the left. The force of it knocked the airplane completely out of control. We rolled hard, almost inverted. I recovered somehow, only to watch helplessly as the airplane pitched up almost vertically and then swiftly back down. Disoriented, I went to the instruments and watched something I'll never forget. The airspeed indicator went from the yellow arc to zero and back, twice, in less than ten seconds. The attitude indicator was tumbling aimlessly. The VSI pegged itself alternately in climbs and descents. The altimeter wound and unwound like a yo-yo. Stars, lights and gray countryside chased each other crazily across the windshield as we pitched and rolled wildly like a chip of wood in a tidal wave. I juggled the controls and the power madly, praying the airplane would not tear itself apart. After several minutes I regained some control, but altitude and heading still belonged to the lessening turbulence. Numbly, I began to realize that the treacherous leading edge of the front was not along the face of those storms, but churning in invisible violence under the innocent-looking cloud behind us.

"Lawrence unicom, 30 is 5 northeast. Advisory."

"Harv, the wind is 320 to 340 at 30, gusts to 45 knots favoring Runway 1. It's really windy. How's the ride?"

"Lousy, Don, give me a wind check once a minute till I get there, okay?"

Closer to the airport, the turbulence slackened, but we were still taking a good pounding. I was exhausted and scared as we rolled out on final, the turbulence increasing again as we descended. I glanced across the cockpit at my front-seat passenger. He sat in rigid staring silence, both hands gripping his seat.

"Wind now 320 at 30." We were really bouncing now, barely under control. I could see from the crab angle as we crossed the threshold that the landing was going to be a real handful. As I wrestled the airplane into a flare, a gust snatched us back into the air. I caught it with power, nosed over, and reapplied full right rudder, lowering the left wing. It was not enough. We pancaked out of control, tires screaming. Snatching the power to idle, I herded the nosewheel back to the centerline from what must have been the barest edge of the runway.

Don was waiting at the terminal, and we quickly helped the passengers inside. I was amazed to find no one hurt. They were pale, badly shaken and awfully thankful to be on the ground. A woman embraced her waiting husband and cried softly.

Quietly, the lobby emptied as Don and I locked up. Outside, we looked for damage to the Six but, incredibly, found none. After we had put away the airplane, I sat looking out at the windy night. Don pulled up a chair and passed a cold beer across the silence. There was not much to say. As I sat listening to the first claps of thunder rolling in the distance, thoughts of cold fronts, fools and little children wandered through my dazed mind.

This pilot learned his lesson the hard way about how a storm feeds and churns in invisible violence many miles ahead of its visible boundaries.

Here's another pilot's tangle with a storm, this time at close quarters. It was a rare encounter in that the airplane sustained damage from a lightning strike—in winter.

My copilot and I were coming home in a Piper Navajo Chieftain. We were westbound, and the evening sky was a clear dark blue, except for a band of clouds forming a barrier ahead. It was nice to see things normal. I don't think I've ever crossed the Cascades during winter without pounding through the billowy stuff. Some days were worse than others, but it was usually bumpy, with ice sticking everywhere. I often wondered if it would ever get so bad we couldn't make it.

We penetrated the white vertical wall and began the familiar bouncing. It was hard work to keep things as comfortable as possible for the passengers. As was normal, we were handed off to approach just as our descent began west of the mountains; as usual, until about 5,000 feet agl, we were bounced, kicked, iced, snowed and, finally, rained upon. Tonight was predictable, except for an extraordinary ingredient added to the soup: the clouds we were flying through were as black as coal-stack smoke. They contrasted sharply with the clouds we had flown through earlier. For a second, I thought about deviating, but where would I go? We were solid most of the time, and besides, the worst I could imagine was a thunderstorm and that was impossible. It was February in the Northwest, and the OAT read −3° C. I felt safe, if knocking off layers of ice with the boots is safe.

But I was wrong. As we passed through the cloud that turned dusk into night, out shot a blinding bolt of light. I couldn't believe my eyes. Could it be lightning in winter, with ice hanging a half-inch thick off the nacelles? But there it was, streaking toward us about twenty feet in front of the nose. My first instinct was to throw up my left arm, covering my eyes and face in desperation. I looked sideways and saw the shadow of my copilot burned against his seat as he squinted at the blazing light. There was no time to react, but as quickly as the lightning appeared it was gone, careening through the aluminum like a rock through a metal drain pipe. We had been struck by lightning, no doubt about it.

I could hear the airplane, along with the passengers, gasping and groaning through the earplugs and headset I was wearing.

The airplane's first reaction was an agonizing roll to the right, as if it were trying to cover up the pain in its wound. And it was hurt. It was hard to determine exactly where we were hit, but after things settled down I noticed the right engine gauges going bananas. The oil pressure was well above redline, and the oil temperature, too, was abnormally high. We were still in the clouds bucking our descent, and I was trying to keep things together and keep the airplane flying.

The first action I took was to call approach and alert them. Before transmitting, I had to hesitate a couple of seconds to allow my vocal cords to settle down, as I could feel them shaking in my throat. "Approach, ORE 404, we've just been hit by lightning, and we're assessing the damage," I said, to the best of my recollection. They came back with standard replies reserved for emergencies, but I could detect the concern imprinted over their transmissions.

Luckily, they were landing aircraft to the west, and, through all the confusion to counteract the roll, we had climbed a bit, leaving only fifteen miles to the runway. With lots of altitude, I kept the power back on the bad engine and soon the oil gauges edged back into more familiar territory. Shortly thereafter we broke out, located the runway, touched down, coasted in and shut down. It was over now, except for everyone's emotions. I felt embarrassed and didn't want to turn around initially; in a strange way, I felt the whole ordeal had somehow been my fault. But I did turn around, and I was greeted by a group of relieved passengers, happy to be on the ground. Everyone looked pale but otherwise normal, and they even lingered a little while, describing their individual reactions and feelings.

My first physical uneasiness came after I got out and conducted the postflight. There was an ugly black hole in the outboard trailing edge of the right elevator. The right prop was completely pulverized, confirming the impact point, with three hunks burned from the trailing edges of two of the three blades. The tips looked as if someone had attacked them with a buzz saw and tried to make them five inches shorter. How they stayed on I'll never know.

The other company pilots walked over to gawk at the damage and to pound us on the back; then the mechanics arrived. They took us back to our hangar, and after describing to the night crew what had happened, I left. It was high time for some real thinking. I had nearly been blasted from the sky by a sneaky, snow-blown bolt of lightning.

Thunder and lightning in winter is not unknown, but damage caused by a lightning strike is rare indeed. The writer was left confused and frightened by the incident, as if the walls he had carefully built around himself had been demolished, leaving him unprotected.

Here's a tussle with turbulence and ice over the Alps that left Winston Churchill, a grandson of the prime minister who led Great Britain through World War II, feeling rather uncomfortable.

The flight in our twin-engine Piper Seneca from London's Gatwick Airport to Samedan, adjacent to St. Moritz, Switzerland, where we spent a winter sports holiday, had been uneventful. The 580-nm flight took 3 hours 40 minutes, and the last hour was spectacular as we flew over 14,000-foot snow-covered peaks in brilliant sunshine to the south side of the Alps. Two weeks later, conditions for our return trip were rather different.

It was mid-January, and a strong, northwesterly airstream was blowing across the entire route from England and across France to the Alps, with winds of 50 knots at 10,000 feet and above.

This airstream was associated with warm-front conditions including layered clouds up to Flight Level 160 over the Alps. Forecast icing was light to moderate above 6,000 feet. With a 50-knot wind on the nose, we would have a groundspeed of only 100 knots and could not reach Gatwick nonstop, so I decided to make an intermediate landing at Basel for fuel.

Traveling light, my wife and I and our three children had the equivalent of six first-class baggage allowances—360 pounds of skis, boots, crash helmets for the Cresta Run, and other winter sporting equipment. Knowing we had 13,000-foot mountains to cross, I was determined not to be above our maximum authorized weight of 4,200 pounds on takeoff from a field that was 5,600 feet above sea level. I therefore loaded the aircraft with only 45 (Imperial) gallons of fuel instead of our usual 79, a weight saving of 245 pounds. In this way, we were 100 pounds under gross weight on takeoff and could be sure of reaching the aircraft's 18,000-foot service ceiling, keeping above the top layer of cloud and any icing problems. Under normal circumstances, the flight to Basel should have been little more than an hour. Counting on a 50-knot headwind, I planned our flight for 1-1/2 hours, allowing a full 1-1/2 hours' reserve to take account of the adverse weather conditions and mountainous terrain.

As we rolled down the runway, which the Swiss Air Force keeps clear of snow throughout the winter, local weather conditions were deteriorating rapidly. Toward the eastern end of the east-west St. Moritz valley, visibility was no more than a mile and a half, and beyond that there was a blizzard.

We were airborne at 1245 GMT and climbed out toward the west over the snow- and ice-covered lakes, keeping clear of the low broken clouds that extended toward the Maloja Pass. As we sought to gain altitude, we experienced extreme wind shear and violent buffeting and were all glad of our diagonal safety harnesses. We had strong downdrafts to contend with, and the aircraft was repeatedly rolled through 30 or even 45 degrees.

We crossed the Maloja at 9,000 feet and, as had been the forecast, the weather was clear over the Italian lakes. Zurich information cleared us to join controlled airspace at Flight Level 140 over the Monte Ceneri Beacon above Lugano, and as we passed 12,000 feet, Minnie and I donned our oxygen masks, leaving the children to curl up and go to sleep in the back. At this point, still on the south side of the Alps, visibility was 100 miles or more, and we could see Lakes Como and Maggiore stretching out beneath us on the left side of the aircraft.

By the time we reached Monte Ceneri at 1315, we had just leveled at FL 140 and were instructed to contact Zurich Radar. Here we turned north to cross the Alps, setting course for the Brunnen Fan Marker 51 nm away. With a groundspeed of 100 knots, we should be there at 1346. As we turned onto our new course, I could see the banks of heavy stratus cloud rising ahead of us to our own altitude, possibly higher. At this point, our groundspeed, according to the DME, which was locked onto Sarrono, was no more than 95 knots, indicating a headwind of 50 to 60 knots. At approximately 1325, to avoid entering the cloud that was building ahead of us all the time, I requested Flight Level 150, which Zurich Radar immediately approved. The climb to FL 150 was laborious—at times the instruments indicated we were *descending* at 250 fpm because of turbulence and down-drafts—and for a period I had to alter course 30 degrees to star-board to avoid entering cloud. When we arrived at FL 150, it was apparent that at least FL 160 would be required to keep us above the cloud. Accordingly, I requested and was granted clear-ance to this altitude. But, try as we might, there was no way we could persuade the valiant 200-hp Lycomings that were now gasping for air to lift us above 15,400 feet. On previous occasions, I had not had trouble reaching the aircraft's ceiling of 18,000 feet. However, I had failed to take into account the extreme lowering of aircraft performance that can be caused by a 50- to 60-knot airstream passing over high mountains. We were not even able to get within 2,500 feet of our usual ceiling. This time there was no way round the bank of cloud that swirled up in front of us. With little more than ten minutes—so I supposed—to run to Brunnen, which was on the north side of the highest mountains and beyond which we would be clear to descend, we entered cloud and found ourselves on instruments.

Soon we were catching ice. The windshield disappeared under a thick layer, and ice was building on the leading edges. Minutes later, the DME locked onto the Trasadigen Beacon north of Zurich. Its verdict was ominous, for it indicated that we still had 24 nm to run to Brunnen and that our groundspeed had fallen to an unbelievable 55 knots. The combination of being close to the aircraft's ceiling in extremely turbulent air and the buildup of ice had caused our airspeed to drop to 110 knots from the 150 knots we should have been maintaining. The headwind accounted for the loss of a further 55 knots. Instead of being barely five minutes' flying time from Brunnen, we were going to need another half hour.

The electric propeller deicing was working well, and the wing and tailplane deicing boots were doing a moderately efficient job of keeping the leading edges clear of ice. But the inboard roots of the wings, the engine air intakes, and the stall-warning indicator probes were all covered in a two-inch layer of ice. The windshield had a three-quarter-inch covering, and there was a five-inch buildup on the outside air temperature gauge.

I was flying the aircraft manually, as the turbulence was far too great for the autopilot to handle. I could no longer expect any warning of an approach to a stall and I was anxious about the low indicated airspeed, so there was nothing for it but to drop the nose and lose altitude. On reaching Flight Level 150, I advanced the propeller and throttle controls to maximum takeoff power in an effort not to lose any more altitude. It was not long, however, before the weight of the ice made it impossible to maintain this level. I contacted Zurich to explain our predicament:

"Zurich this is Golf-Juliet-Bravo. Unable maintain Flight Level 150. Request Flight Level 140. Revised estimate for Brunnen 1410. Have moderate load of ice and groundspeed of 55 knots."

The Zurich controller came back promptly, if somewhat laconically, "Golf-Juliet-Bravo, this is Zurich Radar. That's not very fast, is it? You are cleared to Flight Level 140." The controller was exemplary in his behavior and prompt in dealing with my queries and requests without bombarding me with "helpful" suggestions or unhelpful questions.

By 1400 hours, I was already having difficulty maintaining FL 140, which was only 500 feet above our safety altitude for this sector. According to the map, the mountains, whose peaks had been barely 1,000 feet below us and hidden by cloud and falling snow, were not as high as we had thought, so I called Zurich again, "Zurich, Golf-Juliet-Bravo. I have ten miles to run to Brunnen. What is my safety altitude at this point?" The controller asked me to stand by for half a minute and came back, "Juliet-Bravo, we have you on radar and confirm you have ten miles to Brunnen—you are cleared to descend to Flight Level 130." With considerable relief, I was able to continue our descent, which was now at a rate of 150 to 200 fpm.

At this point, with the worst of the high peaks mercifully receding behind us, a new problem began to engage my attention: we were fast running out of fuel. From Brunnen there remained 60 nm to Basel. Sixty nm at a groundspeed that had picked up slightly to 60 knots meant another hour of flying. We just did not have that amount of fuel. The combination of a groundspeed little more than half the 100 knots flight-planned and the requirement to go to maximum takeoff power—at which we were burning fuel at 23 gph instead of the normal 15—meant that the 1-1/2 hour reserve I had allowed for the trip was rapidly evaporating.

A quick check of the map showed it was only half as far to Zurich, and Zurich Radar confirmed that the airport, despite a low overcast, was above limits with a visibility of 4,500 meters.

By now I was over the Brunnen Fan Marker and reported to Zurich Radar, "Golf-Juliet-Bravo. Brunnen 1410, Flight Level 130. Diverting to Zurich. Request further descent." Zurich: "Juliet-Bravo. Cleared descend to 12,000 feet. QNH 1028 millibars. Contact Zurich approach now."

On our first contact with Zurich Approach, I informed them, "Approach, Golf-Juliet-Bravo. Short of fuel. I have a heavy load of ice. Groundspeed 60 knots. Would appreciate no delay." "Juliet-Bravo, this is Approach. Cleared descend to 8,000 feet, QNH. No delay expected." The half hour flying to cover the 30 nm to intercept for Runway 16 at Zurich seemed interminable as we ploughed through the blizzard. Eventually, as we descended through 6,000 feet and were turning to intercept the ILS, there was a sudden crunch. The one-inch covering of ice on the windshield miraculously slipped upward and back, to smash with a resounding thud against the tailplane. From then on, bits of ice were dislodging themselves on all sides with metallic bangs and jarring noises.

Suddenly, the low clouds parted and there ahead of us was the most welcome sight a pilot can see: like a giant, brilliantly lit, horizontal Christmas tree, there were the runway approach lights. We touched down at 1435 after a flight of 1 hour 50 minutes, with 6-1/2 gallons of fuel in one tank and 5 gallons in the other—20 minutes of flying at full power. An hour later as I checked the aircraft prior to continuing our flight to Gatwick, slabs of ice were still sliding off and smashing on the tarmac.

When, that evening, I wheeled the Seneca into the hangar at Gatwick after an uneventful subsequent flight, the Laker Airways engineer on duty at the time, on hearing about our minor local difficulties, exclaimed, "Nice to be on terra firma—the firmer it is, the less terror!"

The author's grandfather was one of the greatest at statesmanship; the author is no novice at airmanship. One by one, the

bad cards were stacking: first the heavy load inside; the stiff headwind; then the hefty load of ice outside; high, jagged terrain close beneath; no more shove in the engines and no more lift in the wings; and, finally, dwindling fuel. The ice and the strong headwind conspired to make Churchill's predicament doubly tricky by slowing the Seneca's progress out of the problem.

Here's a pilot who found himself in a similarly frigid sky, but without the benefit of radio. Snowfall, mountains and Mooney Mites do not mix readily.

It is snowing. Not hard but thickly, the kind of snow that softens streetlights, turns the golf course into a toboggan run overnight, and seems to hold the world in a kindly embrace when seen from a window.

I am an anachronism in this snow, a whirring, frantic bug whose summer metabolism is out of place as I flail and circle in this fluid combination of cold air and frozen water. I circle and circle, trapped in this mason jar of snow, but I have not yet surrendered to the sharp solidity below or the gray chloroform above.

I am flying a Mooney Mite, a single-seat aircraft, above a mountainside east of Jackson, Wyoming. My altimeter reads 9,500 feet, and the ground is not much lower. At the most I can see half a mile. I have no radio.

I have a small refuge here this afternoon: a plateau perhaps a mile on a side, a rolling bench of lodgepole pine and grass, rutted by one dirt road, which is now snow-covered. I circle this flat place repeatedly, ripping small rents in the peace of the snowfall. Like a plastic yellow and blue PT-19 on a pair of strings, I go around and around dogmatically, aware that should the strings of this sadly vague contact with the ground part, I will hurtle away upside down and conclude myself in a mess of broken rubber bands and wings.

At the end of my strings, where the boy holding them would

be, are three small houses. It is November, and they are, of course, deserted. From my altitude of 200 or 300 feet, they seem faded, stippled on the field with a dry brush, but they offer me slightly more encouragement of survival than does the naked cabin of the Mite. A semistraight patch of road, about 1,000 feet long, doglegs beside them.

I am boxed in. A faint line of cliffs below marks the canyon of the Gros Ventre River, an exit I tried a moment ago. The snow seemed thicker there. Eastward is the ridge I left two moments ago in sunshine. It is 10,000 feet high. There is pressure in my brain: I must land, I must land.

I drop the gear and circle again. I have no indication of wind direction; it is roughly capricious. Without contemplation, I am now turning final. I don't need to remember carb heat; it has been on since I entered the snow. The snow on the road seems very deep, smoothing out the rough edges of the ground as if the earth had been hand-rubbed. I am hesitant, 100 feet high. Should I pull the gear back up and sled the plane in? Is the wind behind me? It pushes me to the right, away from the road, and the Mite's small rudder is ineffective in a slip. I approach the ground. I feel no fear, no anticipation, just sadness.

How did I get here? Is there something greatly significant about my predicament? If I may pay with my life here, there must be something of great importance to be purchased. Surely I have made a vast error to be now facing the choice between a cliffside and an empty cabin at 9,000 feet in midwinter. What basic tenet of flying have I flaunted, or is it more subtle? What flaw is there in my being that draws me inexorably toward this moment of raw survival? Am I, like the suspect witch, being tested against nature? If the coals burn my feet, if the snow swallows me, is my guilt proved?

At Worland, Wyoming, two hours ago, I asked flight service for Jackson weather—4,000 broken, 8,000 overcast; slight deterioration forecast. Later, over Dubois, Wyoming, the sun was shining, though there was a sweep of cumulus over the mountains toward Jackson and snow showers along the ridge. The pass looked sufficiently open, and no doubt I would find, as I have before, that the snow was a light narrow band along the highest peaks. It was not so. I slipped over the ridge, led on by glowing phantoms saying, "It's clear over here," until, leaving me trapped against the slope, the phantoms faded into uniform obscurity, and I circled and circled and planned how to land.

I am gliding, twisting toward the road. It is not right, this approach, I am overshooting my spot, and my gear, I am sure, will grab the snow and throw me. But I still have fuel and power, so with a tang of desperation creeping into my calm, I advance the throttle and leap toward the Gros Ventre gorge, and, deserting my houses, pursue another phantom glow into the canyon.

As I descend, the indefinite ceiling seems to drop with me, but now I find I have three remaining factors in my favor: I know precisely where I am (this canyon will spew me out at the Jackson Airport); there is no ice; and now that my decision is made, my mind is clear to cope with the execution.

The canyon winds, and I have to make steep turns in turbulence, but it widens, and suddenly I pass hard over two men in a pickup feeding hay to cows. Neither of them admits my presence with a look. Cowboys are supposed to be immune to hallucinations. Then I am over the Gros Ventre slide at the mouth of the canyon, and I am safe. I have been here by car, and I know the road. The canyon ends; I cross an old strip and decline it with undeserved confidence, and here is the Jackson Airport, sketched in snow-faded charcoal at the edge of the national park.

I am half an hour late on my flight plan. Flight service thanks me for the call. Inside the FBO's office, warm and bright-lit against the pale darkness outside, a young instructor looks up from a magazine. He has heard my conversation on the phone. "Came over the hill?" he asks, and then, without waiting for explanations I am reluctant to give, he continues, "I don't know I'd really call that VFR."

I stand at the window. I walked on the coals, and I was not

consumed. But I am neither absolved nor convicted. It was not a trial, just another day, and now it is ending, that's all. Significance? I made a small mistake today, and although I will remember it for years, it was not large. I was just the soldier in the night camp who, in his smugness, unaware of the enemy sprawling awake beyond the perimeter, lit a cigarette.

How many pilots have "slipped over the ridge, led on by glowing phantoms saying, 'It's clear over here,'" only to find themselves trapped as the phantoms fade? It is a dangerous practice, described (less poetically) in the accident reports as "continued VFR into adverse weather conditions."

The pilot in the next tale overreached himself, too, while trying to maintain VFR in Alaska. He wasn't fully aware of how far over his head he'd gotten until he turned to his thirteen-year-old nephew, who observed, "We're going to die, aren't we?"

It had been four days of 100-foot ceilings, fog, rain or drizzle. It appeared we would be weathered in another day on Montague Island, a remote roadless area in Alaska's Prince William Sound, 130 miles southeast of Anchorage.

My thirteen-year-old nephew, Rick, and I were salmon fishing. We had landed my Piper Pacer on a beach beside an excellent salmon stream. A large high-pressure area had given us clear skies for our first day, but the next morning the rain and fog arrived. After four days, we were limited out on fish, a bit damp, and ready to head home. However, the weather made safe VFR flying impossible. I had no ADF or AM radio, and the nearest FSS and VORs were out of range, so we could get no weather reports.

Three other fishermen were waiting in a nearby Forest Service cabin for a local charter outfit from Seward (75 miles west along the coast) to fly them out. They had been scheduled to leave Monday. The weather had not allowed it. Now it was Wednesday and the weather hadn't improved. I considered taking off and heading for Seward during one of the brief periods of improvement. I had 2-1/2 hours of fuel, but was reluctant to try it without en route weather reports since I was not familiar with the terrain or weather trends.

I was lying in the tent listening to the rain when I heard a distant engine. As the airplane approached, the rain began to increase in intensity. The de Havilland Beaver landed in a downpour, and I hurried to pick this stranger's brain for weather info.

The pilot assured me it had been good all the way from Seward, with 800-foot ceilings and good visibility until he rounded Cape Cleare on Montague, where things began to deteriorate. So, apparently, the poor conditions were hanging along the south side of the island only. I asked about squalls. He had seen none prior to reaching us, and reasoned that they must have gone over the island and stayed farther north in Prince William Sound. The overall picture was of low-pressure areas moving in continual succession from the Gulf of Alaska. This meant the weather could change rapidly and we should get out quickly. We didn't.

No one was ready to go. It took the other party an hour to get packed. A couple more rain squalls moved through. The other pilot said he didn't like the looks of those since they were increasing in regularity, but he decided to fly out anyway. He showed me, on the sectional, some good beaches to land on along the way to Seward just in case we needed them. He said to keep in touch on 122.9, loaded up, then took off into another squall. I watched him round the cape to the west, keeping ahead of the main body of clouds and rain.

Rick had been out fishing when the Beaver came in, so we weren't ready when it left. Ten minutes later, it was raining too hard. Another fifteen minutes found some good open airspace. The Beaver would have been in Seward by then.

We took off. As we rounded the cape, ceilings did rise, but a squall line ahead moved to block our path. This is where I blew it. I thought about going back to wait for another day. But then my flight plan would be overdue; search-and-rescue would be alerted; and I needed to get back to work. I reasoned the Beaver must have made it (I couldn't raise anyone on 122.9), so it was probably all right once we squeezed past that squall. I went for it.

It is twenty miles from Montague to Cape Puget on the mainland with a string of smaller islands between, so we were always within gliding distance of land, even with the low 600-foot ceilings. The rocky coastlines looked inhospitable. About halfway across, another squall became visible, moving from open sea to the mainland. This was disconcerting because it indicated that the weather pattern had changed in the last hour and a half. I would have gone back, but when I looked behind, the way was closed.

I needed to make it past that advancing squall to get to the beaches the other pilot had shown me. I soon realized we wouldn't beat the weather to the coast, but perhaps we could fly through it. As we flew into it, the rain increased in intensity and the gray shadows that were mountains on our right faded until visibility was almost nil. It looked still darker ahead. I was down to less than 100 feet above the water. A 180 was in order quickly before I lost all visual contact or hit something ahead.

I headed back to the islands and circled them, looking for places to land. There were none, only rocky crags and steep, tree-covered slopes. Montague was still isolated by the dark squall, with no sign of clearing. So we had the back door closed and the front door closed. This left the two side doors: with open sea to the south, Prince William Sound to the north was the only viable alternative. I could still see distance that way. Surely I could find a beach to land on. Ten minutes later, there were no beaches and another door slammed shut as squalls came across

Montague, dropping into the narrow strait we occupied. Now what? I realized I had made a serious mistake when I flew past that first squall. I had never seen weather like this. Apparently these squalls were a prelude to a wide advancing front, not the scattered individuals I was familiar with. Another 180 back to the islands. More squalls were moving in from the open sea. There was no place to go. The weather toward the sea had become nearly solid. The airspace we inhabited was over open water, with menacing mountains on three sides, and the advancing squalls were making it smaller by the minute. Fuel was down to less than two hours. Rick turned to me and cried, "We're going to die, aren't we?"

That was a shocker. I had been so busy, the thought hadn't occurred to me. I became aware he might be right. I lied, "No, everything is cool. Just relax, we are going to be all right." I don't think I reassured him, but at least he didn't panic.

I decided foremost to remain calm, for with that comes the only hope for survival—reason. Reason says: assess the situation, look for alternatives. Pick the best alternative, but remain flexible.

Assessment. I am a 400-hour VFR pilot in a remote radioless area (I had already tried 121.5 and all VORs nearby). I was under low ceilings over open sea, fairly low on fuel. There were no good places to land. The weather in Anchorage and Homer was clear three hours earlier. I needed to get on top for that to help. There were no holes. The area I inhabited was getting smaller.

Alternatives. One: keep circling and hope something clears before it becomes solid IFR or we run out of fuel. Does not look encouraging. Two: crash-land on a rocky, tree-covered island. Chance of survival—moderate at best. Three: ditch on the edge of the coastline. The water is about 35° F. Life expectancy in the water is around 30 minutes maximum, provided we aren't knocked unconscious and can get out of the airplane. Chance of survival—minimal. Four: head out to open sea on a course to Homer's VOR and hope that the tops aren't too high, that there is no ice, and that I can maintain control of the airplane without turning and slamming into the mountains. I have a full gyro panel but only one navcom and very little hood time (none since my last biennial nearly two years before). Not one of those alternatives was appealing. Fuel and time were becoming a factor. I made the decision. ''We're going to climb out of this.''

I asked Rick to monitor my airspeed and call out if we fell below 70 mph. I dropped to 100 feet above the water so I could have my climb and course established well before entering the clouds.

With climb speed at 80, on course and everything trimmed, we were suddenly in solid. Keep the scan going, light control pressures, use rudder and trim, no sudden head movements. Pay attention: you've been staring at the artificial horizon too long, the DG says you made an 80-degree turn to the north; that's heading straight for the mountains, ease back around. Rick called, ''It's 70 . . . now 65.'' Okay, a little forward pressure, not too much, relax a bit, back to 70, 75, 80, back on course, keep it centered, keep up the scan. Thank God there's no turbulence. This is crazy! What am I doing here? I wish we weren't so heavy; we are climbing only 300 feet per minute. Five minutes elapsed, ten minutes, fifteen, as the altimeter slowly turned to 2,000 feet, 3,000, 4,500. Still the VOR was dead, nobody answered 121.5 or 122.9. I would sell my mother for an ADF.

Twenty minutes and 5,500 feet. It looked just as dark as it had at 1,500. Suddenly Rick called, ''Look, you can see the ground!'' Resisting the temptation to peek, I asked him if there was any place we could land. ''Yeah, I think so.'' I glanced to my left and, glory be, there was a hole open clearly all the way down. Better yet, there was a piece of beach down there. I couldn't tell how rough it was or how long, but it looked as if we could probably live through a landing. There was only a second to make the decision: tops elusive, unknown; radios dead; weather ahead unknown. I could lose control of the aircraft any time. We must descend. The hole looked big enough.

I put the airplane into the steepest possible spiral, watching the airspeed closely: around once, twice, oops, into the clouds; now out again just as quickly, getting too fast, ease the yoke back, shallow out the turn but not too much or we'd be in the soup again, around and around. Altitude was fading fast now. The hole got bigger, then we were out of it at 500 feet. I couldn't believe it; there was a beach four or five miles long. It was rocky but wide and not too steep. A quick glance showed more of those demonic squalls moving in fast; we had gotten ahead of the front. There was turbulence, with a brisk onshore wind. It was raining lightly. One pass as we lost altitude.

I picked the smoothest landing site. I wanted to get down before those squalls hit. I needed to be slow for the rocks, but I needed speed for that gusty crosswind. I used half flaps and 60 mph. The rocks were bigger than I thought—I was glad to have those 8.50 tires. I was sinking too fast, so I added some power. We were touching down now, a little bounce and drift, touching down again, rolling, now slowing fast. I brought more power in to get the Pacer as far as possible from the water; the tide was coming in. Full power, then suddenly we were stopped short by a big rock. The nose dipped and I yanked the power off. We were down.

Rick was ecstatic, wanting to know how I remained so calm. Now I noticed I was sweating and that my hands had begun to tremble. I had a headache. It had been the longest twenty-five minutes of my life.

As I scanned the sectional, I found our beach; we were right on course and only twenty-five miles from Seward. My hands were shaking too much to pat myself on the back. We had to wait 4-1/2 hours for the weather to break. When we finally got to Seward and taxied up for gas, the Beaver's pilot was very glad to see us. He said he had been quite worried; he'd barely made it himself.

Weather can change quickly when low-pressure areas are on the move. Although it's often necessary to go up and take a look at the weather before taking decisions, the important part is never to let the back door close behind you. This pilot had doors slam on him in all quadrants. Being boxed in by weather is one of the most uncomfortable events that can befall the noninstrument pilot.

But, of course, there's always that beach—as this pilot found, too.

I rolled my little bird up on one wing and looked down. Sure enough, I could see a house through the hole. There was no fog or lower layer. Happy as a clam and just about as smart, I chopped the throttle and dropped through the hole.

I had flown from Los Angeles to San Francisco the day before, flying an airplane I'd built myself. It was basically a Taylorcraft, but not really, and it had all the instruments of a bicycle—no radio, a compass that may have been calibrated at one time, an oil pressure gauge and a tachometer. What more did anyone need?

At the time I was flying charter out of a small Southern California field, mostly flying Beech 18s or Bonanzas, but my little bird was fun. Normally on a trip by myself I'd have taken something to get me there and back a little quicker than my homebuilt, but this time there was no urgency and I just wanted to enjoy myself. The trip up was great. No clouds, smooth air, and I didn't have to explain to anyone that those two needles weren't supposed to point in the same direction and, no, the engine always sounds that way.

I landed at San Carlos on the peninsula. It was a small, friendly strip where no one was inclined to get upset about an airplane waggling its wings and begging a green light from the tower. I stayed overnight at a friend's house, and the next morning I was bouncing down the strip as the sun came up. Everything looked good until I cleared the tops of the hills to the west and saw a solid cloud layer just below the hill tops. With no weather briefing, no radio, and not enough instruments to get me to the corner drugstore, what I should have done is obvious. I should have executed a 180, gotten to a telephone and checked the weather south.

What I did was settle in my seat, squash the little tickle of alertness by thinking about all the hours I had boring through weather, and bumble on south through the clear air under the blue sky. That was mistake number two. Number one was leaving the ground in the first place without checking the weather. All the way south, weather gathered and thickened under me. I was now flying over scattered to broken clouds. To the west, solid cover was still packed up against the mountains, spilling through canyons and over saddles into the inland valley I was following.

Everything ran out at Santa Ynez, a little town northeast and across the Santa Ynez Mountains from Santa Barbara. The cloud was still scattered, but when I crossed the mountains there was solid undercast. As far south as I could see there was nothing but an occasional mountain peak. I milled around briefly and then retreated to a grass strip at Santa Ynez. On the ground I wondered what to do. Actually, I was now cleverly planning mistake number three. The only person in sight was a man cutting grass with a small tractor, and our communications broke down quickly once we got past "*Buenos días.*" I was stuck until a Cherokee popped down through the overcast and parked next to me. Two amiable business types started unloading their luggage. They told me Los Angeles was solid, but that there was 1,500 feet under the overcast. Great! I could find a hole, drop down through the undercast, and have more than 1,000 feet of comfort between the ocean and me. I could just follow the coast down, pass the Santa Monica Mountains and swing into Santa Monica Airport. So I fired up and briskly put mistake number three into operation.

Up over the mountains again I followed the ridge south, looking for a hole. The first couple I saw showed nothing but another layer underneath. Finally, I hit one that went all the way through. It wasn't very big, but I could see a house at the bottom. In fact, the hole wasn't big enough to fly through or even circle down through. I dropped into it in a turning slip, nose high and canted up to the right.

That was when I realized that, yes, it is possible to fly down an elevator shaft. The hole just went down and down without breaking open, and that house was getting bigger and bigger. At the last possible second I broke into the clear and found myself flying in the foothills over Santa Barbara. I knew I was low as I scuttled down the foothills, but I really got the picture when first a telephone pole and then a line of eucalyptus trees whipped by. I couldn't climb, because the cloud level was dropping as the hills dropped. When I finally got out over the harbor—where there weren't any more poles or trees—I circled for a few minutes to get my breath. I had plenty of fuel and my pulse was only 260, so I figured my troubles were behind me.

My first thought was to go north past the university and land at Goleta. That suddenly became impractical when the clouds hit the water about half a mile north. Okay, there's a farmer who has a landing strip just above the beach a few miles south. That didn't work either. I was in a little pocket in the fog 100 feet or so high and a mile or so in diameter.

The tide was out, there was a long, totally empty beach in front of the Santa Barbara Biltmore, and all of a sudden it looked awfully good. I dragged it a couple of times to make sure it wasn't booby-trapped with ditches or hidden people, then dropped down on the hard sand just above the water. I don't know where the people came from. When I touched down there wasn't a soul in sight, but by the time I had dragged my little airplane up into the soft, dry sand, there were about 30,000 very impressed people crowding around me. Among the welcoming committee were three or four policemen, who were not at all impressed, and a photographer from the local paper who wanted me to put on my helmet and goggles and let him take a picture of me diving frantically out of the airplane. I was even too depressed to tell him I had left my helmet and goggles at home with my white scarf.

It finally cost about $300 to get a pair of mechanics from Goleta to bring a flatbed and some tools, pull off the wings and haul the airplane back to Goleta for reassembly. Strangely enough, I didn't get a ticket from the police (maybe they couldn't think of a charge) or a visit from the FAA representative.

Mistake number four was going back to work at my home base. It was the first time I realized everybody in aviation in Los Angeles read the Santa Barbara paper. Every one of them had clipped the story to pin on the bulletin board.

Experience can be a bad thing when it squashes ''that little tickle of alertness'' to the point of leading the pilot into a sticky situation. But equally, as is evident in the next confession by a cocky copilot, experience and its calming influence can salvage almost hopeless prospects—like zero/zero at airports all around, and fumes in the fuel tanks.

It happened sometime in 1965, in Germany. I was a copilot, so I knew everything there was to know about flying, and I was frustrated by pilots like my aircraft commander. He was one of those by-the-numbers types, no class, no imagination, no ''feel'' for flying.

You have to be able to *feel* an airplane. So what if your altitude is a little off, or if the glideslope indicator is off a hair? If it feels okay, then it is okay. That's what I believed. Every time he let me make an approach, even in VFR conditions, he demanded perfection. Not the slightest deviation was permitted. ''If you can't do it when there's no pressure, you surely can't do it when the pucker factor increases,'' he would say. When he shot an approach, it was as if all the instruments were frozen—perfection, but no class.

Then came that routine flight from the Azores to Germany. The weather was okay; we had 45,000 pounds of fuel and enough cargo to bring the weight of our C-124 Globemaster up to 180,000 pounds, 5,000 pounds below the maximum allowable. It would be an easy, routine flight all the way. Halfway to the European mainland, the weather started getting bad. I kept getting updates by high-frequency radio. Our destination, a fighter base, went zero/zero. Our two alternates followed shortly thereafter. All of France was down. We held for two hours, and the weather got worse. Somewhere I heard a fighter pilot declare an emergency because of minimum fuel. He shot two approaches and saw nothing. On the third try, he flamed out and had to eject.

We made a precision radar approach; there was nothing but fuzzy fog at minimums. The sun was setting. Now I started to sweat a little. I turned on the instrument lights. When I looked out to where the wings should be, I couldn't even see the navigation lights 85 feet from my eyes. I could barely make out a dull glow from the exhaust stacks of the closest engine, and then only with climb power. When we reduced power to maximum endurance, that friendly glow faded. The pilot asked the engineer how we stood on fuel. The reply was, ''I don't know—we're so low that the book says the gauges are unreliable below this point.'' The navigator became a little frantic. We didn't carry parachutes on regular MATS flights, so we couldn't follow the fighter pilot's example. We would land or crash with the airplane.

The pilot then asked me which of the two nearby fighter bases had the widest runway. I looked it up, and we declared an emergency as we headed for that field. The pilot then began his briefing.

''This will be for real. No missed approach. We'll make an ILS and get precision radar to keep us honest. Copilot, we'll use half flaps. That'll put the approach speed a little higher, but the pitch angle will be almost level, requiring less attitude change in the flare.''

Why hadn't I thought of that? Where were my ''feel'' and ''class'' now?

The briefing continued, ''I'll lock on the gauges. You get ready to take over and complete the landing if you see the runway—that way there will be less room for trouble with me trying to transition from instruments to visual with only a second or two before touchdown.'' Hey, he's even going to take advantage of his copilot, I thought. He's not so stupid, after all.

''Until we see the runway, you call off every 100 feet above touchdown; until we get down to 100 feet, use the pressure altimeter. Then, switch to the radar altimeter for the last 100 feet, and call off every 25 feet. Keep me honest on the airspeed, also. Engineer, when we touch down, I'll cut the mixtures with the master control lever, and you cut all of the mags. Are there any questions? Let's go!'' All of a sudden, this unfeeling, by-the-numbers robot was making a lot of sense. Maybe he really was a pilot, and maybe I had something more to learn about flying.

We made a short procedure turn to save gas. Radar control helped us get to the outer marker. Half a mile away, we performed the before-landing checklist; gear down, flaps 20 degrees. The course deviation indicator was locked in the middle, with the glideslope indicator starting its trip down from the top of the case. When the GSI centered, the pilot called for a small power reduction, lowered the nose slightly, and all of the instruments, except the altimeter, froze. My Lord, that man had a feel for that airplane! He thought something, and the airplane, all 135,000 pounds of it, did what he thought.

''Five hundred feet,'' I called out, ''400 feet . . . 300 feet . . . 200 feet, MATS minimums . . . 100 feet, air force minimums; I'm switching to the radar altimeter . . . 75 feet, nothing in sight . . . 50 feet, still nothing . . . 25 feet, airspeed 100 knots.''

The nose of the airplane rotated just a couple of degrees, and the airspeed started down. The pilot then casually said, "Hang on, we're landing."

"Airspeed, 90 knots . . . 10 feet, here we go!"

The pilot reached up and cut the mixtures with the master control lever, without taking his eyes off the instruments. He told the engineer to cut all the mags to reduce the chance of fire. *Contact*! I could barely feel it. As smooth a landing as I had ever known, and I couldn't even tell if we were on the runway, because we could only see an occasional blur of a light streaking by.

"Copilot, verify hydraulic boost pump is on, I'll need it for brakes and steering." I complied.

"Hydraulic boost pump is on, pressure is up." The brakes came on slowly—we didn't want to skid this big beast now. I looked over at the pilot. He was still on the instruments, steering to keep the course deviation indicator in the center, and that is exactly where it stayed.

"Airspeed, 50 knots." We might make it yet.

"Airspeed, 25 knots." We'll make it if we don't run off a cliff. Then I heard a strange sound. I could hear the whir of the gyros, the buzz of the inverters, and a low-frequency thumping. Nothing else. The thumping was my pulse, and I couldn't hear anyone breathing. We had made it! We were standing still!

The aircraft commander was still all pilot. "After-landing checklist, get all those motors, radar and unnecessary radios off while we still have batteries. Copilot, tell them that we have arrived, to send a follow-me truck out to the runway because we can't even see the edges."

I left the VHF on and thanked GCA for the approach. The guys in the tower didn't believe that we were there. They had walked outside and couldn't hear or see anything. We assured them that we were there, somewhere on the localizer centerline, with about half a mile showing on the DME.

We waited about 20 minutes for the truck, not being in our customary hurry, just getting our breath back and letting our pulses diminish to a reasonable rate. Then I felt it. The cockpit shuddered as if the nose gear had run over a bump. I told the loadmaster to go out the crew entrance to see what happened. He dropped the door (which is immediately in front of the nose gear), and it hit something with a loud, metallic bang. He came on the interphone and said, "Sir, you'll never believe this. The follow-me truck couldn't see us and ran smack into our nose tire with his bumper. But he bounced off, and nothing is hurt."

The pilot then told the tower that we were parking the bird right where it was and that we would come in via the truck. It took a few minutes to get our clothing and to close up the airplane. I climbed out and saw the nose tires straddling the runway centerline. A few feet away was the truck with its embarrassed driver.

Total damage—one dent in the hood of the follow-me truck, where the hatch had opened onto it.

Then I remembered the story from *Fate Is the Hunter*. When Gann was an airline copilot making a simple night-range approach, his captain kept lighting matches in front of his eyes. It scared and infuriated Gann. When they landed, the captain said that Gann was ready to upgrade to captain. If he could handle a night-range approach with all of that harassment, he could handle anything.

At last I understood what true professionalism is. Being a pilot isn't all seat-of-the-pants flying and glory. It's self-discipline, practice, study, analysis and preparation. It's *precision*. If you can't keep the gauges where you want them with everything free and easy, how can you keep them there when everything goes wrong?

All Systems Not Quite Go

Flying is hours of sheer boredom interrupted occasionally by moments of stark terror—at least, that's how some pilots see it. One of the most entertaining ways of keeping the mind sharp during those hours of sheer boredom is to contemplate how, right now at this point in space, one would deal with various types of stark-terror moments. The possibilities for spicing up this mental game are as limitless as the player's imagination, because there are hundreds of things that *might* interfere with the uneventful completion of the flight.

For the vast majority of the hours pilots spend in airplanes, none of these things ever does break, burn, burst, bind or give any bother at all. Engine failure is probably the most frequently contemplated misfortune, but in reality the incidence of an engine's quitting cold of its own volition is extremely low. Usually, the cause is some form of starvation, perhaps of fuel or oil or air, or maybe even of decent maintenance. But how often has it been thought, "Hmm, if the engine quit now I'd really be in trouble"?

Much more frequent than engine failures are systems failures—of the alternator and vacuum pump in particular. They are insidious failures that can creep up unnoticed on the inattentive pilot. The longer an alternator failure goes unseen, the fewer the options available to the instrument pilot when he does finally realize what he is missing. Two of the incidents related in this chapter center on electrical failure in single-engine aircraft; each pilot, faced with different circumstances, had a different way of getting down.

Complex though our airplanes might be, they don't come close to the complexity of the nut behind the wheel. He occasionally suffers systems failures, too, and they can be no less challenging. In the first tale, however, we find a pilot faced with an immediately dire emergency—smoke in the cockpit and a fire beneath his feet.

I always gave three reasons when asked why I wore a parachute when flying the glider-club towplane: midair collision, structural failure and in-flight fire. Only the first seemed to me a legitimate concern; the Florida Gold Coast is a high-traffic area and I recently had two near-misses in one day. I just threw in the other reasons for good measure, since I was certain they wouldn't happen in modern lightplanes. The *real* reason I wore the parachute was that, after twenty years of jumping, I felt naked without it.

A fall day was turning into a good one for soaring. Puffy white cumuli were forming in the clear sky, and hawks and buzzards were already circling overhead. From habit, I strapped on my old air force surplus backpack and waddled out to the Pawnee crop duster, which was our glider tug. During the engine checkout I discovered that it ran roughly on the right magneto. It purred on both mags, so another member and I concluded that a spark plug was carboned up. We tried to clear it by revving up the engine and leaning the mixture, but the airplane kept skidding on the damp grass. I decided to clear the plug by taking the Pawnee up without a glider and climbing at full power.

I taxied onto the runway and eased the throttle fully forward. The 180-hp engine pulled the red-and-white crop duster down the grass strip and into the noonday sky. I set up a 70-mph climb at full power to burn the carbon off the fouled spark plug. At 500 feet, I turned left over the Everglades. The engine was running smoothly on both magnetos at 2,625 rpm. I planned to reduce power when I reached 3,000 feet, let the engine cool slowly, and return. Four club members were patiently awaiting me.

At 1,500 feet, the roar of the engine suddenly quieted. I quickly scanned the instruments: the tachometer showed 2,000 rpm. I wheeled the airplane back toward the airport so that I could make a dead-stick landing if the engine quit completely. Then, as abruptly as before, the engine roared back to full power. A few seconds later, it lost all power and backfired furiously. The waiting club members heard the noise and peered skyward at their returning tow plane. A thin mist was streaming out from the fuselage. I was down to 1,100 feet just south of the airport when I smelled a sharp, lung-burning odor. Smoke! I quickly lowered the flaps to steepen my descent; I was going to land this crate as quickly as possible and *run*.

The smoke was now rapidly filling the cockpit and it occurred to me that I might have to jump. At the same time, I worried that I might be overreacting—just think of the embarrassment and expense if I bailed out unnecessarily!

By now I was well below 1,000 feet. The smoke was thick, stinging my eyes and burning my lungs like acid, when I suddenly felt intense heat. No question about it now—the airplane was burning and I had to get out. As I took my hands off the controls and opened the right side of the cockpit canopy, I could see shimmering heat waves coming up over the front of the right wing. Simultaneously, the Pawnee pitched over into a shallow dive.

When the door swung open, suction pulled the heat from the raging fire beneath my feet up into the cockpit. As the blast hit me, I instinctively lunged outward—but I couldn't move. In my near panic, I had forgotten to release my seat belt and shoulder harness. I was forced to turn away from the cool air and face the searing heat roaring up at me. I groped for the belt release among the parachute buckles, ripcord, and other straps at my waist. I grabbed the release and, in one motion, pulled hard and vaulted my body with its 30-pound parachute out of the seat. I sailed out past the trailing edge of the wing and realized I was very low. I was falling feet first as I grabbed the ripcord and pulled. I just lay there in the rushing wind, wondering which would come first—impact with the ground or the opening jolt of the parachute.

The fully opened orange-and-white parachute looked beautiful as its lower edges gently fluttered and snapped. Then something else caught my eye. Off to my right and above me, my stricken craft was in a death dive. I could see the extent of the fire now and I had no doubt about the wisdom of my decision to jump. Bright orange flames were gushing from the vicinity of the engine and gas tank. It was a stunning sight.

I was drifting backward, and as I struggled to turn the parachute, I heard the airplane crash with a loud FOOM! It had sheared off the tops of several Australian pines and dived into the ground almost vertically. Suddenly, I, too, was crashing through treetops. I hit a large limb with my backside about the time the chute spread out over the branches like a big tablecloth and brought me to a halt. I ended up sitting on the limb 15 feet off the ground. The foliage was dense, and as I blindly hung there listening to the airplane burning and exploding just a couple of hundred feet away, a new fear welled up in me. Would the forest fire arrive before I could get down from the tree? I heard voices above the crackle of the fire and yelled. As they zeroed in on my voice, I unfastened my parachute harness. They helped me down and led me out of the thick underbrush.

The airplane didn't make out too well. The tips of both wings were high in the trees, the engine was a foot in the ground, and the smoking wreckage was totally burned. The framework was twisted and broken, and there were numerous puddles of molten metal on the ground. As the local fire department put out the last traces of the grass fire, my eyes fixed on the bare seat springs where the cockpit had been.

The FAA investigator arrived and we speculated about the cause. There were two prime candidates: either a fuel line broke and was ignited by the backfiring, or the engine backfired up through the carburetor. The wreckage was too mangled to offer any real clues.

I was wearing Bermuda shorts and a T-shirt, and I noticed that the hair on my left arm and leg was singed off, my eyebrows and lashes were singed and I had a scratch on my leg from the tree landing. My left elbow was red and it hurt. All things considered, I got away clean.

Fire, fortunately, is one of the rarer emergencies for pilots to ponder. The smoldering Pawnee is probably now at the top of the author's list of reasons for wearing a parachute. For the rest of us, who fly without parachutes, the best protection is a well-maintained airplane and a thorough knowledge of what to do if fire does break out of the engine. Things can happen fast.

Here's a tale of three vacationers and an old Bonanza leaving the Florida sun and returning north to Buffalo, New York. Unlike the tug pilot and his near-instant calamity, these three had a problem that is often missed for many precious minutes: generator failure—with daylight fading fast and an undercast beneath.

We left Fort Lauderdale, Florida, on Monday, bound for Buffalo, New York. John's 1958 Bonanza was a good machine, with decent radios and a nice-sounding engine, so I dozed occasionally in the right-front seat as we proceeded northbound. We dropped in at Charleston, West Virginia, for more fuel and another weather briefing. Buffalo featured its customary overcast and snow showers, which were forecast to remain for the rest of the day—and probably the rest of the month.

"Can I keep following our route on the sectional?" Mary asked. She liked flying and picked up a good deal of knowledge about it. She sat behind me and had been following the course of our flight through the rear window.

"Well, for a while you can. We ought to run into a low overcast about the middle of Pennsylvania. Tops about 7,000. We're filed for 9,000. Buffalo's got 1,500 overcast, 4 miles with snow. A heavy west wind. Forecast is for up-and-down conditions in snow showers." She nodded. We hopped back in, John cranked up, and we were off, IFR at 9,000.

Two hours, thirty minutes until generator failure.

The flight droned on, and we settled deeper into our seats. John was doing very well, and the airplane was also turning in a superb performance. The low white rug of overcast had slid beneath us as we crossed Franklin, Pennsylvania. It reached as far as we could see. Sunset was about an hour away. Rochester, New York, was our alternate. Its weather was 800 and 3 in snow. Buffalo was down to 700 and 2. On we flew.

Forty minutes until generator failure.

As John began the descent for the approach, tops were at 7,500, with light rime ice in the clouds. We were northeastbound, over the lake, setting up for the ILS approach to Runway 23. Special weather, now 300 obscured and half a mile in heavy snow. The wind was 270 at 25 to 35.

Generator failure.

We leveled at 4,000. The icing had stopped, and the air was just slightly bumpy. I fiddled with the number-two VOR receiver to get a cross-check, but its needles sat motionless.

"Damn thing. Out again, huh?" John commented. We had had trouble with this radio before. The ADF bearing showed us directly abeam the outer marker on the north side, still heading northeastbound.

"You are number two," the radio crackled, "behind a United flight, just approaching the ma . . ." Fade out. His voice hollowed, as if it had run into the end of a long tunnel. Then it was gone.

The panel lights faded next. Then the gas-gauge needles sank to their empty marks. We had just about an hour of fuel remaining.

"What . . . what's happening!" John exclaimed. I could feel Mary stirring behind me. The electrical gauges were on the left side of the panel, behind John's knee.

"Generator and battery!"

"Dead!" he answered, flipping the switches. The artificial horizon and directional gyro were vacuum driven.

"How . . . ?"

"Have you been checking the ammeter?" I asked.

"I . . . no!"

"Neither have I. Give me the wheel."

I held the column-release latch as he swung the controls over to me. The Bonanza wobbled a little but then straightened out. I pulled the power back to slow down. Darkness was only minutes away. The clouds outside were dull and heavy gray. Our gas was limited. The thought of being back above the overcast, lost, at night, was a horrifying sensation. This was the last moment that I'd know our position for sure. I knew the area very well. I had lived and flown there for many years. I began a right turn toward the inbound ILS heading.

"The United flight?" John said, gesturing toward the darkening murk outside the window.

"They'll get him out. They'll see us turn on radar." I took a cut into what I knew the wind would do to us. I felt strangely confident, on the stick, with it, together.

"Don't worry," I announced in a calm voice.

"Okay," Mary responded. I could feel her breathing on my neck and could sense her pushing her hair back with her hand. I pulled more power off and began a letdown.

"Everyone look for the ground." I was going for ILS minimums—200 above the airport, 923 feet msl. I knew there'd be nothing out here we could hit. If we didn't see anything at minimums, we'd climb on top and head south—until we ran out of gas.

"Straight down! The ground!" Mary yelled at 1,000 feet indicated. The ground whipped by, 200 feet below. I pushed a little lower. "Look for something." We flew. I turned 10 degrees more to the west. The clock ticked by 1 minute, then 1-1/2, then almost 2. It was quite dark now, the cars below had their lights on.

"Get ready. I'm going to land."

"Where?"

"Anywhere. It's getting too dark. I'm turning into the wind."

"Wait! The school! Our school. We just passed it."

"Are you sure?"

"Yes. Yes."

I knew where I was. I turned more to the west. Ten, twenty, thirty seconds of vague terrain. Then the road. The highway. It would lead to the airport. It swung beneath me as my hands wrestled the airplane to a new heading. Then the glow of the approach lights appeared ahead. And the runway.

"John, crank down the gear." I did a tight circle over the approach lights. "Down!" he yelled, pointing to the mechanical arm. I rolled out of the turn, put the runway beneath us, then chopped the power and flared. Buffalo International Airport. We taxied to the ramp in silence, as the tower followed with a flashing green. John called them on the phone. "Congratulations" was all they said. They wanted nothing more. We patted each other on the back and then went for a drink. Two drinks at least.

The flight had been instructive, after all: a sweaty lesson about keeping one's scan on *all* the instruments and another about the hazards of faulty batteries.

When all else was gone, unconventional navigation—even as blind as that described here—had to be preferable to running the tanks dry IFR at night. But had the generator failed over strange territory, a different plan of action would probably have been required.

Here's a pilot who had a similar problem away from home base; he approached it on a different tack and came down the long way.

It was the first day of the air traffic controllers' strike. I called Cleveland Flight Service to inquire about general aviation departures and got a busy signal for the next ten hours. Finally an FSS specialist told me that limited handling of general aviation IFR flights would begin Tuesday, the second day of the strike. What does "limited" mean? I asked. Come out to the airport and take your chances, was the reply. It sounded as though we could be stuck there for days.

On Tuesday, I called Cleveland Flight Service at 5:00 A.M. to try to beat the busy signal. The specialist answered on the first ring, gave a weather briefing and took the IFR flight plan. "Good luck," he said, just before hanging up. At 9:00, we were on the ramp loading the Rockwell 112. After a fifteen-minute wait, we were cleared as filed to Wilkes-Barre, Pennsylvania, and soon took off and climbed to 7,000 feet. The chatter on departure and center frequencies sounded reassuringly normal. In the back, Mark (one of my two passengers) settled down for a nap.

It is apparent to me now that clues to my upcoming problem were there by midflight. I had only to put them together to get the message: electrical failure. First, somewhere between Clarion and Keating Vortacs the DME quit. It simply dropped out, refusing to give time, distance or groundspeed displays; it stared back at me with only an incandescent decimal point. That's high-tech for you, I thought. The fanciest instrument in the airplane is the one that fails. I responded by ignoring it. It was fairly easy to overlook, because I didn't really need the DME.

Second clue: while tracking Victor 226 eastbound from Keating, a published course of 090 degrees, the aircraft entered a gentle right turn and flew off the airway southbound. The autopilot was loyally following the number-one nav, which appeared to have lost its mind. I disengaged the autopilot tracking, flew back to the airway and delegated the navigation to number two. We tracked V-226 without further problem, and number one now seemed to be giving good on-course indications. Why had it led us astray? I didn't know, but I decided to keep both navs tuned on the airway so I could check them against each other.

Third clue: as we approached Williamsport, I left center to query flight service about our destination weather. I made several transmissions and got no reply. This was especially puzzling because Pittsburgh Flight Watch has a remote transmitter at Williamsport and should have yielded excellent reception. Then an "obvious" answer suggested itself: the controllers' strike had forced the FSS specialists to spend all their time answering phone calls from general aviation pilots.

When I returned to New York Center, I couldn't raise anyone there either. A look at the chart showed that we were closer to the North Mountain transmitter, so I called center on 132.6 and got an immediate, strong reply. The controller politely chided me for the interruption, saying that he had instructed me earlier to change to the new frequency. I had heard no such transmission, but thanked him all the same. Why the breakdown in communications? Again, the controllers' strike provided an explanation. The supervisory personnel manning the center were a bit rusty.

Each clue had presented itself, then slid by unnoticed. Instead of seeing the underlying pattern, I regarded the clues as unrelated events and developed a rationalization for each. Meanwhile, the alternator was working only intermittently (as I learned later), and, unnoticed by me, vital energy was draining from the battery.

The hand-off to Wilkes-Barre Approach immediately yielded a descent to 6,000 and a left turn to 050 degrees, vectors for the ILS approach to Runway 22. Wilkes-Barre was reporting a 200-foot ceiling with visibility 2 miles in fog. As we motored outbound, communications with Wilkes-Barre Approach became increasingly garbled. Finally, I looked down under the control wheel and read the electrical system's epitaph: the ammeter was showing deep discharge and the voltmeter was showing 9 volts. Nine volts! No wonder the radios refused to work. Suddenly those earlier clues fell into a meaningful pattern, and for the first time I knew I was dealing with the situation my primary instructor had warned me about eighteen years ago: VFR flight above a solid overcast. I cycled the alternator switch and punched the circuit breakers. No change. My grip on the control wheel tightened. I was angry at the radios for what they had done to my plans, angry at that disgusting 9-volt reading and mostly angry at myself for not catching it sooner.

It was then that I turned off all the radios. It was a gratifying action, a gesture of retaliation. Only the transponder remained on, still squawking 6740, because it might help the controllers keep other flights away. My intent was to shut everything down in the hope that the charging system might replenish the battery enough to operate one radio.

The effect was a psychological liberation. I would no longer squander my attention on trying to talk to people on the ground, or on spinning the OBS. A lot of theoretical solutions to my problem—an ILS approach and an ASR talk-down—were eliminated. For the first time I relaxed. The problem wouldn't be as tough, I thought, if I were orbiting over my home airport near Baltimore, over the Delmarva Peninsula, an expanse of table-flat land between the Chesapeake Bay and the Atlantic Ocean. The highest terrain is about 40 feet, and the clouds seldom reach to the ground. A chart suggested another suitable area. The farmland of southern New Jersey is just as flat and only about 120 miles away. Allowing 1.6 hours to get there, that leaves us with about an hour to loiter over Wilkes-Barre. The plan of last resort snaps into focus.

I will continue circling for a while in hope of somehow getting into our intended airport. When about 90 minutes of fuel remains, I will proceed at max-range power settings to southern New Jersey. The blind letdown will be in straight flight at minimum comfortable airspeed, say 65 knots, gear and flaps down and harnesses tight. Even if we never break out of the clouds, we can reasonably expect to leave a long furrow in some potato field. If we do break out, the Atlantic coastline can serve as a navaid. Not a bad plan, I feel. So how shall we spend the next hour?

"There's a farm and a road down here," says Dan, pointing

out the right window. We bank right for a better look. The hole in the cloud is about two miles in diameter. The throttle comes back and we spiral down to take a look.

There is a neatly kept farm with a large pond, a winding road, an intersection with a smaller road. Out comes the sectional. I suspect that we are south of Wilkes-Barre and scan the map for these landmarks. There they are. Winding roads and ponds. But the important thing is the view beyond the farm. To the north the land slopes upward into a narrow valley; to the south it blends into foggy haze; to the west a mountainside disappears upward into the clouds. It's a sucker hole. Mixture rich, prop and throttle forward, we climb out of the hole into the sunlight. Power back to slow cruise, we turn northbound, scanning the cloud deck for more openings. Small holes come and go. After ten minutes we turn southbound, trying to stay over the same general area.

We're about twenty-five minutes into our hour of grace, and the ammeter needle has been parked center scale for some time, neither charge nor discharge. I take a guess that the ADF has the least power consumption and switch it on. It is tuned to Crystal Lake, the missed-approach fix. The needle swings to the ten-o'clock position and wavers back and forth a bit. Hit the test button and slew the needle around, release. It returns to ten o'clock. All right! We'll fly directly to Crystal Lake—at least then we'll know our exact position. More breaks in the clouds.

"Look, there's a VOR." Sure enough, Dan has spotted the Wilkes-Barre Vortac, framed by a generous-sized hole in the clouds. Spiral down, check the sectional. This is even better than Crystal Lake. The airport is only a few miles away, due north. I've traversed this area before and know that there is only one ridge separating us from the airport. The visibility is not too bad here, about four to five miles. We're actually VFR. We should be penetrating the Wilkes-Barre control zone about now, but I assume that approach has continued to track us on radar. A touch of back pressure, and we clear the ridge about 200 feet from the ground and 100 feet from the clouds. We bank to the right toward the airport, but see only haze. Off with the ADF, on with the VOR, all digits glowing brightly. We're on the 350-degree radial, so the airport must be there. We continue northeastbound with about 1-1/2 miles visibility, and three runways materialize from the haze.

We enter a downwind for Runway 22, and I depress the flaps lever. The flap motor grinds for about two seconds and then quits. No electricity equals no flaps. The flaps are stuck with about 5 degrees of deflection. I put the landing gear down, then turn left base. The gear-down indicator lights are dark, but that makes sense—no electricity, no light. Watch for traffic. The tower gives us a flashing red light. No landing yet! Then the memory of the grinding sound hits me.

The hydraulic pump in the aft fuselage makes a characteristic grinding sound as the gear goes down, and I heard no such sound. No electricity means no hydraulics means no gear. *That's* why the tower controller waved us off. I pull the emergency gear extension. This is supposed to be a free-fall system.

"Is the landing gear down?" Mark asks.

"I don't know. I think it is. Aren't you glad this is a rental airplane?" We turn base and watch the tower. Green light. Final approach a bit faster than usual for the small flap deflection; let the speed bleed off just above the runway, flare, flare. We make a gentle touchdown on the wheels. There is no other traffic moving and we motor past the passenger terminal, find a parking space near the Pocono Airways repair facility, and shut the airplane down.

Had I taken the proper steps?

I could have looked at the ammeter more frequently during flight. The mechanic later discovered that the alternator diodes were functioning intermittently; I suspect that the alternator was on its good behavior when I looked at the gauge. But during a two-hour flight I looked at the ammeter twice, while I had scanned the flight instruments perhaps 200 times. I vowed to expand my scan pattern and, except during instrument approaches, read the engine and electrical gauges whenever I scan the flight instruments. There were other lessons. When something fails in flight, look to the source, and look for the patterns. If two devices fail, look for what they have in common. And then there is the question of the controllers. I had used them as scapegoats for some of my problems, when in fact, even in the depth of the strike crisis, they had performed flawlessly.

There were also some things we did right: foremost, we carried plenty of fuel and didn't plunge into an immediate attempt to land. Some in-flight problems are solved by immediate action, others are exacerbated by it.

It was time to have a chat with the people in flight service. Facing the FAA was easy compared to the events of the past hour. The specialist listened to my tale of an unorthodox approach and then telephoned the tower to ask if the controllers wanted to talk to me. The answer was quick and short: no.

''Who's in the tower during the strike?'' I asked.

''Two supervisors and three trained monkeys,'' replied the specialist.

''Well,'' I said, a bit giddily, ''tell the controllers thanks and give the monkeys an extra banana.'' Dan grabbed my arm and pulled me out of the office.

Some in-flight problems demand instant solutions; others, such as this one, can be better solved by slower, deliberate exploration of all the options. The immediate task was to shut everything off and preserve what little electrical juice was left, before figuring how best to use it. Well stocked with fuel, he had time on his side.

In the next mechanical malfunction, the pilot kicked himself for not conducting a more thorough preflight. It's surprising what can be missed by a casual or hurried walk-around. But then, who would think of looking for mud dauber nests?

It happened on a typical Alabama summer afternoon, complete with blue sky, scattered cumulus and haze topping at 4,000 feet. My boss, Lou, asked me to fly him to Tuscaloosa, Alabama, to negotiate a paint job for his Aztec. I was delighted to put paperwork aside in favor of flying. I'd recently acquired a 1968 Cessna 150; it was my first airplane, and it was beautiful, so the most transparent excuse would send me rushing to the airport.

After the walk-around and run-up, Redstone Tower cleared us for takeoff. Moments later, we were airborne.

"Huntsville Departure, this is Cessna Two-Two-Niner-Niner-Seven, off Runway 35, Redstone, maintaining runway heading, climbing to 6-point-5, going to Tuscaloosa, VFR, negative transponder."

"Two-Two-Niner-Niner-Seven is radar contact, turn right, proceed on course, and climb to en-route altitude, caution, restricted area."

We turned right 180 degrees and flew south over the city of Huntsville as the 150 slowly and steadily gained altitude. Crossing the Tennessee River, we topped the haze and soon were straight and level at 6,500 feet, on top.

Flying VFR at low altitudes on an Alabama summer afternoon can be dismal, if the lack of visibility doesn't make it downright dangerous. But if you can get on top, the view changes from dull to dynamite! Most of the 130-mile trip was pleasurably spent sandwiched between a bright blue sky and clusters of white puffballs in a nest of gray haze. The little 100-hp Continental was velvety smooth at 2,700 rpm, and we covered ground at a decent 101 knots. Although Lou's class of aircraft was far more exotic than anything I'd flown, Niner-Niner-Seven was a solid ship, in beautiful condition, and I was proud to show her off. He sensed this and flattered my ego with nods of approval when appropriate. My confidence in the plane was total.

Fifteen miles northeast of our destination, we began our descent. All was well as I enriched the mixture and began to throttle back. As we maneuvered around the friendly cottonlike puffs and entered the gray murk, the engine began to splutter and falter. I'd never had an engine-out, and I looked at Lou, who just sat there, arms folded, looking back at me and smiling like a Cheshire cat. He obviously understood the situation and was playing the flight instructor, waiting for the novice in the left seat to pull himself together and solve the problem. Then it occurred to me—of course, carburetor ice! The airplane immediately responded to carburetor heat and we both had a good laugh, punctuated with bad jokes about the need to change trousers.

Just below the cloud level, our laughter was replaced by the sound of the breeze blowing across the aircraft. The prop was only windmilling. The lifeless engine failed to respond to my attempts to restart it. I was shook, but in the back of my mind, I "knew" that Lou had another lesson for me to learn. This time, though, my glance wasn't greeted with a smile. Lou, the old pro, was calling "Mayday" over the mike.

Just north of Tuscaloosa the terrain leaves much to be desired for anyone contemplating a landing. Our eyes darted across the miles of timber growing on the rugged, hilly ground. Then, from the corner of my eye, I spotted a little patch of relatively smooth terrain. I remember muttering, "It's not much, but thanks, Lord, I'll take it." I glanced at the altimeter: 3,000 feet and unwinding. It surprised me that things were happening so fast! I hoped I had enough altitude to fly a full, standard pattern (I suppose that even under stress, I'm a creature of habit), so I lined up for a downwind approach. We'd been listening to Tuscaloosa Tower since we'd started our descent, but we seemed to be too far away to reach them with our transmitter. Our Maydays went unanswered. Lou switched to 121.5 as I turned base.

"Mayday! Mayday! Cessna Two-Two-Niner-Niner-Seven, engine out, approximately fifteen miles northwest of Tuscaloosa. We're trying to reach a pasture but it looks doubtful."

I wished he hadn't said that. It looked promising to me. Lou was used to flying aircraft much heavier than mine and didn't realize that our glide would reach as far as it did. Our Maydays still went unanswered. We were about 200 feet agl when we realized that our end of the field was a succession of steep hills; not too promising, but we'd have to make the most of it. In spite of my best soft-field efforts, we struck the top of a hill with bone-jarring impact. Ricocheting off the hill, we stalled, fell onto the other side, rolled 100 feet down the hill through a creek and slid, sideways, halfway up the next hill, spraying mud, water and grass all the way. I wish I could have been a spectator, standing at the side of the pasture, watching this pair of clowns scare hell out of a few cows and themselves. When the airplane came to a rest, we laughed, congratulated each other, kissed the ground and heartily cussed the airplane.

A short hike to a nearby farmhouse got some of the rubber out of our legs, but we were still shaky as we telephoned Dixie Air in Tuscaloosa, explained our predicament and asked that an A & P man be sent to discover the source of our difficulty.

While we were waiting for help to arrive, I remembered that a week earlier, a lineman at Huntsville Aviation had told me that my fuel tank vent opening was blocked, probably by mud daubers, those lovable wasplike creatures native to the Southeast. They build their nests with soft, wet dirt that, when finished, hardens like concrete. After reaming the vent with a coat hanger, I made a mental note to watch it carefully. On this day, though, I couldn't recall paying any special attention to the vent during that quick, robotlike preflight.

When help arrived, my suspicions were confirmed. The vent opening was packed solid with mud and insect larvae. An hour later, it was cleared. I asked that the airplane be inspected from prop to tail to determine if it was airworthy, while I wrestled with the next decision; should I fly it out?

The field was a hilly pasture containing a number of grazing cattle. It was shaped like a dog leg with approximately 1,500 feet on either side of the bend. One end of the field dropped off 50 feet then rose to form two additional 50-foot hills. The other end was relatively flat. The entire pasture was covered by a carpet of grass 2 feet tall, and it was surrounded by trees and telephone wires.

After pacing the level end of the field, we determined that there was ample room to take off and clear the obstacles. I felt that if I emptied the airplane of all unnecessary items, drained a few gallons of fuel and tried it alone, I could fly out safely. Lou was happy that I was electing to go it alone. He again paced the field and established a shutdown point. If I wasn't airborne by the time I passed him, I was to abort. We backed the plane to within inches of the downwind fence, locked the brakes, made a careful run-up, lowered 10 degrees of flaps, firewalled the throttle and released the brakes.

The airplane accelerated, but not fast enough. It hit a bump, bounced and settled again. I broke out in a cold sweat as I horsed it off the ground a few feet in front of Lou's position. The stall warning was blaring, and I knew I'd never clear the tree line ahead, but by now I was going too fast to abort! I banked left, following the dog leg and saw, from the corner of my eye, my left wingtip clipping grass. I glanced at the airspeed indicator—40 mph indicated. There was that tree line again! The stall warning was screaming, but there was nothing I could do but try to clear those trees. It was either over them or into them, and in a state of near panic, I pulled it up and over the treetops with only inches to spare.

An experience like mine would be nothing more than material for hangar flying were it not for the lessons I learned.

First, my preflight had become mechanical. I looked at those things I habitually checked, but seldom saw what I was looking at. I'm sure I glanced at and touched the fuel tank vent opening, but I didn't really check it. I didn't realize the possible consequences resulting from a blocked vent. With a gravity-feed fuel system, there must be some means of pressure equalization or the engine will draw a vacuum in the fuel tanks and choke off the fuel supply.

Second, I learned the importance of always knowing exactly where you are. When we realized an emergency existed, we declared our position as fifteen miles northwest of Tuscaloosa. Once on the ground, we learned that we were northeast of the city. Fortunately, no one had to search for us.

Third, I learned that even in a little Cessna, when the engine quits the airplane comes down fast. It's important to practice forced landings, for your decisions must be correct the first time. Know your engine-out procedures as well as you know your call sign; *unlike* your preflight, these procedures need to be automatic.

Fourth, the takeoff distance over a 50-foot obstacle listed in the owner's manual may not apply to a grassy field on a hot August day. I knew that. I wonder why, when it really mattered, it didn't occur to me.

If this pilot was bugged, you might say the next one was plugged. And it wasn't his airplane that broke, but rather the pilot himself. Just as nature abhors a vacuum, so does the human ear not take kindly to separating high pressure from low pressure.

On long trips I usually wear earplugs because I've always thought that long exposure to engine noise can affect your hearing. They don't do any harm; the radios are just as audible and engine noise is muted, so why not?

I was flying from McAllen, Texas, to Islip, New York, with

stops at Houston and Knoxville, Tennessee, in a turbocharged, nonpressurized Cessna 402. Having taken off from Houston and engaged the autopilot, I inserted the plugs while climbing, and leveled at the assigned 17,000 feet. About three hours later I landed at Knoxville, removed the earplugs and deplaned. Refueling, a leg stretch and a cup of coffee were in order.

Half an hour later I was airborne again, climbing to 17,000 and having trouble engaging the autopilot—too busy to fool around with earplugs. But soon after I had leveled at 17,000, the recalcitrant autopilot engaged, so I settled back and inserted the plugs. Three hours passed uneventfully before I descended into Islip.

While taxiing in, I reached up to remove the left earplug. Agonizing, excruciating pain stung my inner ear when I pulled to extract it. I tried again, very gingerly, and once more my ear's core radiated tear-jerking pain.

The light dawned. I ceased further efforts to take the plugs out until the airplane was parked and shut down. Inserting the plugs, unpressurized and at a high 17,000 feet, had effectively sealed about half a vacuum next to my eardrum; I was now at sea level with a big pressure differential on each side of the plugs.

I wriggled, twisted and finally removed the left plug as gently as possible. Its inside was coated with blood, more of which oozed from my ear. The time was about 2:30 A.M., and the OAT was about 10° F.—hostile circumstances. I was deeply concerned but decided to pull the other plug. For fifteen or twenty minutes I eased, twisted, coaxed and, finally, agonizingly, removed the right plug. This one was clean.

How stupid of me not to have anticipated the debacle. Once I had identified the potential consequences, surely a climb back up to altitude for removal would have been in order. I should have done that.

That afternoon I saw an ear doctor, who determined that both drums had hemorrhaged. He said that everything would probably straighten itself out, but that the affected areas could deteriorate, resulting in perforated eardrums—a serious condition that might involve corrective surgery.

No treatment was recommended. I just had to wait and see if natural healing would save my bacon. It did.

No doubt about it, a climb back to altitude would have been the most painless way of removing the earplugs. But, on the other hand, would he have been any wiser to have climbed back into the airplane while racked with pain?

The three crewmen aboard the Navy S-2A in the next story didn't feel too smart either, even though they did manage to get both engines running again.

One of the great and final admonishments given by instructors and friends is to leave your troubles on the ground. Taken into the cockpit, personal worries and woes can be fatally distracting.

It was the day after JFK was shot, and our minds were running high and hard on the events in Dallas. We were approaching the spot where we'd been when the fatal shots were fired—7,500 feet over Alice VOR—in the same aircraft, a rather bedraggled Navy S-2A that belonged to a Corpus Christi advanced-traning squadron. My thoughts ranged over commissions; painting my boat; my old collie, who was expecting pups; and the balky aircraft heater I had fruitlessly tried to light dozens of times yesterday and today. Anything to avoid focusing on the death of a president on a street a few hundred miles away, even as our flag had swung from "to" to "from."

"Discrete, discrete, discrete," the UHF had crackled suddenly. Deke, Jerry and I had stared at the overhead radio panel, as if it would give us a sign. The radio had stared back in dumb plastic silence, the unattached voice in our headsets continuing. "All aircraft this frequency maintain radio silence and return to base."

"What the heck?" I asked no one in particular. Jerry and Deke shrugged their shoulders in unison, and we pointed the stubby-nosed old bird back to Navy Corpus.

Now, twenty-four hours later, repeating the simple, dull exercise, foggy-minded and remembering, we watched the flag again begin its wiggle. There was little conversation on the intercom as Jerry rode left, Deke right, I the portable jump seat in between.

"Stand by to mark on top," Jerry broke the spell quietly through his boom mike. "Rick, you want to try the heater again?"

I had the feeling he was reaching for a comforting word. Perhaps I was witnessing the first sign of calm courage that would win him a Navy Cross in Vietnam, just before he was blown to a wisp of smoke over Haiphong Harbor. Jerry was directing our attention to the job at hand. Once more I cycled the gasoline-heater switches while we bundled against the unseasonal cold in nonregulation woolen gloves and turtlenecks, like ancient Jenny jockeys.

She quit without a sputter, bark or backfire. There was a minor shudder, then total silence as the two three-blade props rapidly wound down to thick blurs. The roar of an icy wind filled the cockpit as the orange nose arced toward Texas, and the panel lights dimmed perceptibly.

For an eternity, no one moved. The peculiar empty feeling one gets when an airplane begins sinking through the sky like a falling leaf filled my insides. Six eyes locked on the airspeed as it descended through 100 . . . 90 . . . 80. . . .

An incredibly calm and sensible voice emanated from Deke's mike. "Jerry, a little airspeed, okay?"

Cylinder-head temperatures: that's what tells you the engine is dead. Manifold pressure and rpm can be deceptive, but cylinder temp . . . both engines were growing colder than a loan officer's heart. Engines *never* fail simultaneously, they had assured us. Except that just now, they had.

Then it was sudden activity. Someone flipped the transponder to the emergency code, and my thumb nearly rammed the ident button through the console. Jerry established a glide of sorts; Deke's voice was icy as he announced to San Antonio Center that a Navy S-2A with three on board, 3 miles and 180 degrees outbound the Alice VOR had lost both engines.

Then I noticed a pale darkness creeping over the ground below. With blackness facing me, I decided to do something. I was surprised at the confidence in my voice. "How about we try to relight 'em?"

"Huh?" Jerry was occasionally a little slow on the uptake. The altitude was now winding through 4,000 and Deke was holding his own with center.

"*Fuel!*" Jerry suddenly exclaimed, the first finally to figure out the single element that would cause a simultaneous failure of both engines. I flipped both selectors from crossfeed to direct.

"Prime 'em," Deke barked, leaving San Antonio to wonder what was happening.

"You've got it," Jerry released the wheel and concentrated on throttle, primer and starter. Number one coughed, then burst to life with a deafening roar. The bird slewed violently to the right, and our hands collided as Jerry and I both stabbed at the single-engine rudder-assist switch. The nose seemed to hunt stability as both men in front overcorrected on the pedals. Deke let go almost as quickly as he had leapt into the breach, and Jerry's voice came tight. "Starting two."

"Ninety knots and level flight." Deke smiled slightly. Number two came alive, and a gingerly rate of climb was established. Jerry resumed control as Deke picked up the conversation with center. We were handed off and received permission to proceed to Alice International and terra firma.

It was on final that I realized how many silent prayers had issued from the cramped cockpit; there are no disbelievers nestled in dark, silent airplanes between two windmilling props. I wondered how three students would explain all this to the skipper and training officer. Of course, the maintenance man would tell us all about contaminated fuel; that we had clogged the crossfeed gate with sludge—or something like that—by flying 3-1/2 hours in the crossfeed mode, thus causing fuel starvation. The same thing would have happened if we had been direct-feeding for that period; switching back and forth, direct to crossfeed, as we were supposed to, probably would have prevented it. What if we'd been more preoccupied or at a more critical phase of the flight when the engines quit? As the lights of Alice came into view, I resolved to leave my troubles on the ground. Somehow flying generates enough of its own.

The crews' brains were disengaged from the business of managing the machine. Lucky indeed were they that the fuel lines didn't run dry on final approach.

In the next discussion, Peter Garrison had an almost opposite problem with brain engagement while flying Melmoth, his late lamented homebuilt. Garrison was so intent on executing the forced landing he thought was inevitable that he ignored a factor that could have kept him aloft until he reached a much more hospitable landing site.

My alternator had failed as I left Los Angeles, but, figuring that one ought to distinguish between frills and essentials, I flew on toward Wichita, Kansas, stopping for the night at Santa Fe, New Mexico, where I had the battery recharged.

The weather report the next morning was unfavorable. Some kind of storm—I have always had a hard time telling an upper-level low from a lower-level high, or a ridge from a trough—was working its way up from Mexico, or down from Utah, and the weather briefers were fabricating all sorts of dire stuff between Santa Fe and Wichita. Reduced as I was to nonelectrical VFR flying, I figured there could be no harm in having a look, so midday found me poking at a wall of fog beyond the Rockies. It didn't look good for going under, so I retreated to Las Vegas, where the clouds began, and climbed above them, then struck eastward again, looking for breaks through which I could descend over lower terrain. As the clouds got higher and no breaks appeared, I became edgy; my lower jaw felt funny and I found myself glancing at the fuel gauges all too often. Eventually, though, after turning well to the south and almost westward, I found a big tear in the blanket and dropped through it.

Underneath, conditions were good: ceilings 3,000 or 4,000 feet above the ground, unlimited visibilities, none of the snow and blow of the forecasts. I followed the highway toward Amarillo, Texas, but then I grew impatient with the detour and turned northeastward across barren terrain.

It was maybe five minutes later that the engine went funny. The roughness was very bad—more than just plug fouling. Obviously something had broken somewhere. I was going down.

This was my second partial engine failure. In the first, I lost the whole left side of my engine after takeoff but the remaining three cylinders brought me around the pattern and back onto the runway in a cockpit churning with smoke. So I knew the feeling: you're sitting about two inches above your seat, and your thoughts are racing like a runaway carousel with the awful organ-grinder music at full blast. What is it? *Stay calm*! What am I forgetting? *Stay calm*! Pick a spot! Air, fuel, ignition? *Calm*! *Calm*!

In a storm of calmness, I reviewed everything. Fuel pressure was okay. Switch tanks. Water? No. Reduce throttle (less strain or damage if it's a piston or rod); enrich mixture. EGT readings were weird, unsteady; I switched through all six and couldn't make any sense of them. Cylinder-head temperatures were going crazy, too; all dropping because I'd reduced power except number five, which was climbing sharply. The problem was obviously in that one. Had I dropped a valve into the cylinder, creating a continuous stream of exhaust gas on the EGT probe?

I had made a 180 the moment the trouble started, and now, losing altitude slowly, I was pondering my landing strategy as I tried to puzzle out the mechanical problem. A meandering dry riverbed below me was my first chance at a workable landing. Should I keep the gear up (belly skins, flap tracks, possibly wing ribs, prop) or lower it (gear, prop, cowling, but maybe save the wings)? I desperately wanted to cut my losses in the homemade airplane that had taken five years to build.

A dirt road suddenly materialized out of the badlands. Good. I would land gear down, and with luck. . . .

I checked the mags. On the left the engine seemed to run smoothly; on the right mag it quit almost entirely. I switched back to both. I was not losing altitude as rapidly as I had first thought. The line of the interstate emerged from the gloom 10 miles ahead, and I checked the chart; there was a paved strip there. If only I could make it.

I made it. The 35-knot wind blowing precisely athwart the runway was insignificant compared to the vast relief of feeling wheels squealing and bouncing down an asphalt runway.

The airport was deserted; so I walked into town through the fierce freezing wind and bought $35 worth of tools at an auto-parts store. I hitched a ride back to the airplane and did a post-mortem. My hands were good for only a few minutes in the chill—I cut and bruised them badly, feeling no pain—but in those few minutes, I found that the problem had been the disintegration of the nylon drive gear in the right mag. Everything else was fine.

The people I was going to see in Wichita sent an airplane down for me; we dropped off the ailing mag at Amarillo, where it was overhauled overnight. The next morning I picked it up, chartered a 150 back to my airplane, replaced the mag, miraculously got the plane started on what was left of the battery, flew back to Amarillo to get the mag timed, then finally began what was to be a seven-hour, belly-to-the-ground, snow-swerving, scud-ducking, gully-running trip home. No fun at all.

Later I got to thinking. An airplane has two mags for redundancy. If one goes bad, you switch to the other. So why did I return to "both" after ascertaining that the airplane ran well on the left one alone? I thought about that question quite a bit. The answer I came to is a humbling one, but its disturbing implications are worth every pilot's consideration.

Basically, it was a stupid mistake. Still, why did I make it? I think I had a certain unconsidered prejudice against running on only one mag. In various situations, people shut off one, then the other, but they always say, "Don't leave it on one too long; it'll foul the other set of plugs." So I had an unreflecting reluctance to run on only one. Of course, I didn't think about any of that at the time; I just automatically switched the mags back to "both," as though that were the only way to fly.

And why did I land at that little strip? Well, of course, I was so grateful to find a genuine paved runway that I might as well have been at the entrance to Heaven. But it would have been a lot more convenient to have flown on to Amarillo. And if I had simply switched to the left mag, I could have done just that. But one mistake led to another.

The basic problem went deeper. Until you've flown for decades in reliable old airplanes and experienced every known emergency, you're pretty much pioneering each time something goes wrong. You're on your own. Time is short. You try to think back over articles and accident reports, hangar flying, the hundreds of rules of thumb you've learned and then forgotten, for the one that will save you. You try to stay calm. But that process has a funny effect on your thinking. You tend to become fixated on any plausible answer you hit upon. Thus, I thought, "I'm going down." I had more or less committed myself to a landing of some sort. When I saw the CHT rise on number five, I thought, "Something's broken in that cylinder." Now I was fixated on a mechanical explanation, so when I did the mag check, its significance did not come home to me. I could have seen easily that the problem was confined to the right mag, but I was locked into the mechanical-failure/forced-landing mode.

Can this be what happens when a pilot loses the engine in cruise, makes a forced landing that damages the airplane, then discovers that he or she had an empty fuel tank selected? Can it be simply that the moment the failure occurred, the pilot switched into the engine-failure/forced-landing mind set, thought only about picking a spot, getting into position and setting up a glide, completely forgetting that there might actually be nothing wrong with the engine?

And then there was, for me, the grimmest thought of all: suppose this had happened on one of the transoceanic flights I'd made in the very same homebuilt. Over the middle of the Pacific or the Atlantic, you while away the hours with mental lifeboat drills. There's a lot to do before hitting the water; don life vests and wet suits; ready ELT, flashlight and raft; put out a distress call. Would I have gone straight into the engine-failure/ditch mode and started that mental checklist, never realizing that I could continue perfectly well on one mag? Would I have ditched merely because I was mentally prepared to ditch?

Probably.

The trouble with having a firm plan is that it might be too firm, masking more attractive options—as Garrison chillingly points out at his conclusion.

Here's a pilot who had a plan of action for a multiengine takeoff. But when one engine quit, he found he didn't have many options, the least attractive of which was to fly straight into a two-story hotel.

Several friends and I had flown down from Palo Alto, California, to Punta Pescadero in Baja, California, in my Navajo.

The trip was uneventful, and we enjoyed the tropical weather and deserted beaches for two days. On the third day, we flew to San Jose del Cabo, took on 650 pounds of fuel, and then continued to the Cabo San Lucas Hotel's 2,900-foot sand strip at Chileno Bay. The landing was perfect, and we proceeded to enjoy coffee and a stroll along the beach.

Afternoon found us back at the airstrip preparing for departure. We were 300 pounds under gross, but an 86° F. temperature, a 3-knot tailwind and a 2,900-foot downhill sand runway all spelled alert. I told my competent single-engine VFR copilot that I wanted to cross the midpoint at 70 knots. This would leave us 1,500 feet downhill with full power—and plenty of room to attain Vmc plus 10. After a textbook start-up, we went through a full-power static run-up on each engine to check all systems. Both of the big Lycomings sounded perfect.

As we lined up at the upper end of the strip, I was intoxicated by the beauty of the dull gold sand runway pointing downhill to the azure Sea of Cortez. Nevertheless, I was tense as we began our takeoff roll. The deep rumble of the big Lycomings was reassuringly normal. We rolled over the midpoint at the planned speed. Full power came up smoothly on both sides. Fuel flow, pressure, all temperatures normal; the copilot called Vmc. And then it happened. The right rudder suddenly came alive, and I felt an undeniable yaw. A quick glance at the engine-instrument cluster confirmed my fears—manifold pressure on the left engine was falling rapidly, rpm was deteriorating.

Instinctively, I knew we could not stop short of the brook bordering the airstrip because of the runway's poor braking surface. We had no choice; we had to take off. Immediately after rotation, I ran out of right rudder, the stall warning sounded and all the electrical annunciator lights came on, indicating a failure of the left electrical system.

"Call out the airspeed, and keep your eyes on the runway," I heard my calm voice say to my copilot. Another voice, this one internal, ticked off the procedure: everything forward, gear up, flaps 15 degrees, cowl flaps up, blueline speed, identify dead engine, confirm, feather.

Soon the yaw settled down to a disconcerting 10 degrees, the stall horn ceased its loud blare, and we were descending nose-up directly toward the two-story hotel. Blueline speed seemed about 6 inches ahead of the needle on the airspeed indicator, and we were full steam on the right engine. My only choice was the toughest one I have made in twenty-three years of flying—push the nose down and reduce power on the good engine.

I had just asked the passenger sitting aft of the copilot whether he had the emergency hatch opening in hand when a wonderful sensation took hold; ground effect. Our rate of descent slowed, stopped, and suddenly we were climbing. As I eased power back to the right engine, we were on the positive side of both airspeed and rate of climb. For the first time since takeoff, I began to breathe.

I made a slow, cautious turn and followed it with history's most careful uphill landing. I suspected the engine had failed because of a crankshaft shear. But a post-landing diagnosis indicated the engine air intakes were partially blocked by a lead-in pipe that had disintegrated. The electrical failure came from a circuit problem unrelated to the intake shutdown.

There had not been a crankshaft failure, and the engine might have continued operating at partial power, but excessive heat surely would have led to an engine fire. I realized I had made the right decisions for the wrong reasons. My cool evaporated and my legs turned to jelly. But we were back on the ground, whole, with a repairable airplane.

Later, we encountered a fellow aviator and his wife who had been enjoying cocktails on the hotel veranda as we departed. He recalled, "I heard those props go out of synch and said, 'Let's get out of here, Millie!' You came within ten feet of converting the dining room into an air museum."

Although I fly regularly, the chief pilot and CFI at my home base had insisted on full emergency-procedure practice every six months. Just before departure for Baja, he had taken me through all the hoops: short-field work, slow flight, maximum-performance maneuvers and engine-out practice under the hood. "Practice, practice, practice," the wise man had told me.

We've all heard the admonitions about the value of the second engine in a twin—it'll fly you to the scene of the accident, and it doubles your chance of an engine failure. By staying current at engine-out handling, however, a pilot can tackle the odds on his own terms.

Talking of engine failures, how about losing it while more than 100 miles from land over the Atlantic and 400 pounds over gross? And all in the cause of catching fish?

Isis and I work as a team, spotting swordfish off the New England coast and guiding commercial fishing boats to them. She's a green and white Citabria, but not your average, ordinary, plain-vanilla Citabria. She's got special navigation and communications gear and carries an extra 65 gallons of fuel in an expensive belly tank—enough to extend her range to over 2,000 miles—and she's certificated in the restricted category at 600 pounds over gross.

On a normal day we'll take off at 6:00 A.M., fly 200 miles out into the Atlantic and rendezvous with the boat. After searching for fish for seven or eight hours, we head back to the beach and land at 6:00 P.M. If you've ever sat in an airplane, any airplane, for twelve hours, you'll understand when I say we know each other fairly well.

September 27 started off just like any other day: we had arrived at the boat around 8:30 A.M., the sky was overcast, and there weren't any fish to be seen. We were flying our standard 750-

foot search pattern, staying within a mile or so of the boat. Flaps were set at 15 degrees, with the airspeed at 60 knots, the big, specially hinged windows open on both sides and the tach at 2,100 rpm to maintain altitude. We'd puttered around the boat for a couple of hours, getting bored, and Isis was still 400 pounds over gross as I joked with the crew on their marine radio.

Quite abruptly the engine quit, although not completely. My rpm dropped below 1,500 and Isis started shaking like a wet dog. We started down—rapidly.

Quick! Mixture full rich, throttle full forward, nose down for airspeed, flaps up for ditching. The shaking got worse and the rpm fell lower. "I think I'm going to join you." I radioed to the crew. "This darn thing just stopped running." Down below, a crew member got a life ring ready, then grabbed his camera. I was down to 600 feet.

Seat belt and shoulder harness tight, glasses off. The sea looked angry, with a 25-knot wind blowing foam off the white-caps. There were no clearly defined swells, just lots of choppy waves. "Not a good day to ditch," I said to Isis, as I reluctantly picked a ditching heading ad planned an approach to the boat. Five hundred feet. "You're trailing a lot of black smoke," the boat crew replied. Black smoke, I thought. Maybe she's running too rich. I cautiously leaned the mixture, afraid of losing what power I had. Four hundred feet.

The mixture knob was almost to full-lean when the engine started to develop power. I leaned further—1,600, 1,800, 2,000 rpm. I played with the throttle, but that only caused her to lose power once more. At 2,000 rpm she was shaking badly; we were losing altitude less rapidly, but we were still losing. Three hundred feet.

The windows! I forgot that they were open, creating tremendous drag. Closing them might keep us airborne, but leaving them open would give me a quick exit in the water. I hesitated for a quick second.

The sea looked really mean from 200 feet. I closed the windows and she flew. Haltingly, sluggishly. But Isis didn't want to get wet either, and she slowly started to gain altitude. We passed the 500-foot mark, and now I glued my attention to the engine gauges. Oil temperature and pressure remained steady as we worked our way up to 1,000 feet, circling the boat. It looked as if she might continue to run for a while, but I didn't dare touch the throttle or mixture as we staggered through the air doing 70 knots. I alerted other spotter pilots to my predicament and received suggestions, advice and encouragement. We diagnosed the problem as a broken valve or cracked cylinder, or both, and I knew the hard part was yet to come.

The nearest land was Nova Scotia, over 100 miles to the north. Mike, another spotter pilot, offered to fly along with me. The two of us left the safety of the boat and headed north. The obvious question occupied my thoughts: how long will she run on three cylinders, 400 pounds over gross? I lovingly patted the instrument panel and spoke a few words of congratulations and encouragement to an airplane that was shaking as badly as I was.

"Mayday. Mayday. Mayday. Yarmouth Coast Guard, this is Citabria 53824, 100 miles south, partial engine failure, squawking 7700." The Canadian Coast Guard was fantastic, acting as liaison between Mountain Radar Approach and ourselves. Within minutes a de Havilland Buffalo search aircraft was en route, and a rescue helicopter was standing by on the ground. Mike was reading maps and giving Loran coordinates, while I concentrated on flying. My clothing was drenched with sweat.

I started pumping my excess fuel overboard, feeling only a slight twinge of guilt for the 100-dollar bill I was dumping into the ocean. Down below, the community of international fishing boats was flashing the word to "Look out for a little green airplane with a rotten motor."

The next hour seemed to take days as Mike, Isis and I flew on, occasionally passing a fishing vessel. It felt good to have someone along for the ride, but I was only too aware that if Isis gave up, Mike could only watch me ditch. For the hundredth time, I checked my raft, survival gear and engine gauges. I worried that the continual vibration might shake something loose. My eyes were glued to the oil pressure.

''Citabria 53824, this is Rescue 91412. We have visual contact with you and the other aircraft at our two-o'clock position; one mile.'' The Canadian Coast Guard aircraft, following vectors from approach control, joined us thirty minutes from land. I thanked Mike profusely as he turned around to go back to work.

Land! But my excitement and relief turned to dismay—flying low over the rocky coastline, I realized that the boulder-strewn fields were as dangerous to land on as the angry sea.

Trying to remember everything I'd ever learned, taught or read, I made a high final approach to Runway 33 at Yarmouth, fully expecting Isis to quit cold as I retarded the throttle. One, two bounces and we were down. A poor landing, but I didn't really care. Isis was still idling, and we taxied up to the customs office and shut down. She made a few terminal noises and stopped.

After a few deep breaths, I managed to get out and walk around to her nose where—to the delight of the helicopter crew and other onlookers—I planted a big, juicy kiss directly on her spinner. ''Thank you, Isis. Thank you very much.'' The prop turned halfway through by hand, and then froze solid. She had given me all she had.

The customs man was quite upset because we had not een expected. It took all my self-control not to laugh at him.

Later examination showed that an exhaust valve had snapped off and rattled around inside the cylinder, destroying the spark plugs and beating on the piston for the next hour and a half. The piston, with two holes in it large enough to put my finger through, would make a good doorstop.

I learned that the best care and maintenance cannot guarantee perfect performance. And when something does go wrong, don't give up: push and pull every knob, control and lever in the cockpit. When your engine quits, you've got nothing to lose by trying everything. If you do get it running, leave it alone and land as soon as practical.

My habits haven't changed. I preflight carefully, change oil when required, and some great aircraft mechanics inspect Isis regularly. But that only satisfied the mechanical, physical side of her. So I still kiss my airplane after every flight, and I still say "thank you." And no one in this world can prove to me that it doesn't help keep both of us safe and dry.

The Beckoning Sky

A large chunk of the reasoning that went behind many pilots' learning to fly was the appeal of being able to fly pretty much anywhere anytime. This was probably the argument put up frequently in reply to the doubts of family and friends while the pilot was learning. Think of the freedom, he said, in being able to fly to the mountains for a weekend of skiing, or to the beach cottage or, well, wherever *we* want to go and still be back for work on Monday morning. The pilot has backed himself into a corner, escape from which will be against his better judgment. He has spent months convincing family, friends and work associates how useful a small airplane can be, but he has forgotten that, without an instrument rating, he lacks the means to keep the promise. He's forgotten about the weather, and pilots who forget about the weather often get a rude awakening. The pressure to fly is great. The sky beckons.

It would be easy to think that the professional pilot is above and beyond such beginners' dilemmas. By and large, he is. But he can fall foul of a different pressure: the evil greenback. When your job depends on whether you fly, judgment can take a back seat to visions of the debt collector, the repossessor, the bank manager. The same pressure to fly beckons you to the sky.

And then there is the bit-of-both pressure from the clock hand that comes when the schedule has gone to pot: a passenger pickup that's running late, an appointment that's almost due, these are the ingredients of the mishap caused by impatience. In the first tale that follows, air-show veteran Duane Cole feels lousy, but the show must go on.

I arrived in San Antonio, Texas, to begin my sixth annual training session with the pilots of the H. B. Zachry Company on the evening of April 20. Company president Bartell Zachry and chief pilot Skip Reed had made five hours of dual aerobatics per year mandatory for all their pilots. It was their contention that after pushing buttons in their Lear, Citation and King Air operation for fifty-one weeks a year, the pilots needed to spend one week flying a stick-and-rudder airplane around all three of its axes.

For the last two years, La Quinta Motel's pilots have joined in the program with the seven Zachry pilots. In the past, I have stayed ten or more days to complete the training, but this year other business deprived me of the luxury of time. So by April 28 I was on my way home with a check in my pocket for 46 hours of dual.

Between air shows and my students, the hectic pace continued: on June 8 and 9, if I included flying to and from Palestine, Texas, to give aerobatic dual to John Copeland's Mitsubishi pilots, I was in the cockpit a total of 11 hours. On June 10 and 11 I instructed 10 hours of aerobatics at home. This was followed by a 4-hour flight the next day to Dumas, Texas, where I was scheduled to fly an air show on Saturday, June 13.

Air show chairman John Maxson, greeting me on my arrival, said he was going to hold me to a promise to spend the night with him and his family, so immediately after securing the T-Craft we proceeded to his home. This suited me fine; it would allow me a couple of hours' rest before going out that evening as guest of the air show directors. To tell the truth, I was so tired I would have been happy to stay home and eat hot dogs with the kids.

After a long day at the airport my hosts were tired, too; the party broke up early. Back at Maxson's and in bed by 11:30, I had no trouble falling asleep, but my sojourn into dreamland was short-lived. At 2:30 I awoke feeling as if I was burning up with fever. Only by taking aspirins twice did I succeed in breaking the fever and finally getting a few hours of sleep.

At the airfield Saturday morning I found the weather less than ideal for an air show. The wind was 35 knots, gusting to 45 with a rising thermometer that would push the density altitude to nearly 7,000 feet by show time.

As waiver time approached, my temperature, which had subsided during the night, began rising again. One of the flying club members was a doctor who kindly offered to drive me to a hospital for a quick examination. His diagnosis was fatigue, dehydration and a slight kidney infection.

I thought about canceling my participation in the show, but, of course, I couldn't. I rationalized that I had come a long way to perform, and to cancel would cost me a lot of money. Above all, it would be unfair to my sponsors and the several thousand people who had given up their day to see me fly.

My first event was a dead-stick routine. This act is begun at 5,000 feet with the engine shut off and the propeller stopped. From there I execute a series of loops, slow rolls and inverted flight down to pattern altitude, where I make an inverted downwind leg. Rolling upright, I continue on to land dead-stick and roll back to my original parking space. I have been doing this act for forty-one years, and 99 percent of the time I end up back in the exact spot where I had been parked. But not this time. For the first time in hundreds of performances, I landed short of the runway.

Embarrassed by such a poor showing, I was determined to go on with my second act and to make it a superb exhibition. Well, it wasn't bad but definitely not superb. Although the audience may not have noticed, my positioning was only fair and I had a heck of a time holding headings on outside maneuvers.

It was a long afternoon, but nothing lasts forever. Eventually the show was over, and with the cooperation of my sponsors I was able to fuel and be on my way by 4:30.

My hasty departure was necessary because of a previous commitment to fly in an air show the next afternoon in Hammond, Louisiana, approximately 1,000 miles away. By hurrying I could make it home, about half way, before dark. My first stop was at Vernon, Texas, where I bided my time for half an hour while the airport manager came from home to give me service. My second stop was made at Luck Field, my home port, on the south edge of Fort Worth. After dodging a couple of thunderstorms, I was still able to land about 20 minutes before sundown. Even though I was feeling miserable, my landing should have been the usual unspectacular event, but it wasn't. Instead it was the worst landing I had made since before solo.

That evening, while my wife, Judy, went into Fort Worth to fill a prescription ordered by the Dumas doctor, I reflected on the day's events and laid plans for the next. I would shoot for a 7:00 A.M. takeoff and make my first stop only an hour away at Palestine, Texas. Then, if I made my next fuel stop at Eunice, Louisiana, I would have enough gas to continue on to Hammond and do my bit in the show before gassing up for the return trip. With any luck I would make home before nightfall.

After a restless night I was awakened at 6:00 A.M. by a booming thunderstorm. Cursing my luck, I made my dutiful call to flight service and got the usual pessimistic response: "VFR not recommended. It won't improve until late afternoon." Despite the gloomy prediction, I continued my preparations to leave. As I suspected, the rain, which ended about 8:00 A.M., was followed by a rapidly clearing sky. My takeoff at 8:30 was an hour and a half later than I had planned, but I still had ample time to make it to Hammond by show time.

The first leg of the journey was without incident, though I did get a bit shook up when I discovered 8.5 Gs registered on my G meter. After an aerobatic demonstration, the recording hand of the instrument never indicates more than 5 Gs, so naturally I was puzzled. Then it dawned on me. Those 8.5 Gs were put there by that horrible landing I had made the previous evening.

Thirty minutes after touchdown at Palestine I was back in the air and on my way to Eunice. After I landed, I taxied up to the gas pump, killed the engine and climbed out of the T-Craft. After two or three minutes of fruitless waiting for a flight-line attendant, I walked to the airport office, only to find it locked. I was doubly disappointed because the shortage of fuel was not my only concern. Remembering the doctor's warning about dehydration, especially with the medicine I was taking, I felt an urgent need for water. Dialing a phone number posted on the door for emergency service brought no better results; evidently the operator had gone to church. It might be a couple of hours until his return, leaving me with the alternative of proceeding on to Opelousas, thirty miles to the east, or missing the show in Hammond. My watch and gas gauge indicated enough fuel to make it to Opelousas, so I decided to go on.

I had to push the airplane a considerable distance to a place I could tie the tail before hand-propping it. Then, wouldn't you know, the pressure carburetor began acting up. For twenty minutes I alternately cranked and turned the prop backward with the throttle open to relieve the flooding. I was really pooped when the engine finally started.

Anxious to be on my way, I hurriedly reset and locked the throttle in the idle position, then went behind the airplane and untied the tailwheel. Shades of yesterday: I had not put enough tension on the throttle lock. By the time I realized the throttle was creeping open, the airplane was beginning to move forward. I dived for the tailwheel, catching it with one hand; with the other I grabbed the tie-down rope. Only with prayer and all my remaining strength was I able to get about six inches of rope around the tailspring. Somehow, with one hand I managed to get a knot in it that secured the airplane until I could adjust and properly lock the throttle.

Not wishing to waste precious fuel, I lost little time getting back into the airplane and taking off. The way things were going, I should have guessed that I would find no gas at Opelousas, either. When I arrived, the place was deserted. A phone call to the police department located someone connected with the airport, but they refused to come service the airplane. By now I was becoming desperate. It was 1:00 P.M., just an hour from show time. My next option was to locate some car gas. While I was dialing a taxi company to ask them to bring ten gallons of no-lead, a young man drove up. He was a life saver. Without hesitation, he drained ten gallons of gas from his Cessna for me. Continuing to be a Good Samaritan, he monitored the throttle while I propped the engine, which started on the first pull. Really pressed for time, I paid the young man for the fuel, thanked him for his kindness and took off.

After I landed and was out of the airplane at Hammond, the most urgent thing on my mind was to find something to drink. In my haste to find some water, I even bypassed the FAA man who came to perform the usual weekly ritual of checking my license and aircraft papers.

My late arrival at 2:20 gave me only fifteen minutes before I was scheduled to fly. With my thirst quenched and papers checked, I was back in the air at 2:35. Surprisingly, my performance went off well. I still felt rotten, however, and still had a 500-mile flight ahead of me. Fueled and off the ground at 4:00 P.M., I felt my luck was changing. A favorable wind got me home before sundown with only one fuel stop.

By the time I landed I was really feeling terrible but, anticipating my condition, Judy was waiting to help put the airplane away and drive me home. I went straight to bed, my temperature climbing. Falling into a fitful sleep, I alternated between chills and hot spells. Shortly after midnight I awoke wringing wet with sweat, but the fever was gone. Feeling pretty weak, I got up and took a shower, then went back to bed to sleep soundly until noon the next day.

In retrospect, I think my guardian angel (all old pilots have one) took care of me through a weekend of continuous stupidity beginning in Dumas with my decision to perform. Had there been a fence or any other barrier short of the runway at the end of my dead-stick act, the results could have been disastrous. The 8.5-G landing I made at Luck Field could have seriously damaged my airplane. With my senses dulled by fatigue, it was just plain luck that saved my airplane in Eunice.

Over a forty-year career, I have never failed to fulfill a contract. I have flown under and around bad weather, when I wasn't feeling well and even when the airplane was not functioning properly, all because of pride, greed and the ridiculous old slogan, "The show must go on." But old dogs and pilots can learn new tricks—in my case, to establish limits of health and endurance and to live by them.

The sky can look deceptively inviting when it's the place to earn the money to pay the bills. And when you're an air-show pilot like Duane Cole, it's not a few passengers you're disappointing if you cancel, but a crowd of thousands.

In the next admission, Steve Wilkinson reasons that since the rest of the pilot population seems ready to confess its aerial transgressions on the ILAFFT page, there's no reason why a Flying *editor shouldn't admit to being a jerk. Wilkinson didn't have a crowd to disappoint, but he did have one important passenger waiting for a ride home in the magazine's 310 from Kennedy Airport. And Steve was running rather late.*

The key to the airplane was on my bureau. I, however, was on my way to the airport. And going back to get the key has put me a good half hour behind schedule. Even then, I have the dim feeling that rushing through preflight—which I am planning to do—is eventually going to catch up with me.

I know the flight will be one of those blizzards of clearance copyings, frequency changes, vectors and approach plates: Westchester to Kennedy, a bare twenty-five miles away, to pick up an incoming airline passenger on a bitter, snowy Saturday night. On a flight like that, you don't even get time to synch the engines before departure turns you over to approach—fifteen minutes of climb, turn, tune, talk and descend.

Flying's Cessna 310 is chocked on the dark ramp in front of the hangar when I finally get there. It is fueled, oiled and ready to go. I grab the flashlight out of the glove box, drain the mains and the belly sump—don't even bother with the aux tanks, knowing I won't use them—and then take one quick lope around the airplane to check the dipsticks and gas caps and count the wings. If I don't get this show into the air, my passenger is going to be pacing the general aviation terminal at Kennedy wondering if it wouldn't have been easier to take the limousine.

The takeoff is sloppy, with me still setting nav frequencies and adjusting the shrieking cabin-air vents as I climb toward the blackness over Long Island Sound.

Turn left to 080 to intercept the Deer Park 332, cleared to 2,000 and expect 3,000 . . . no, cleared to three now and call Kennedy Approach 127.4, report reaching.

I tell Kennedy Approach that I'm level at 3,000 and haven't had time to get the ATIS.

"Oh, don't worry about that—I'll get it for you."

Isn't that nice? There's so little traffic on this Saturday that Kennedy controllers, used to a polyglot pandemonium, are positively expansive with goodwill.

Approach asks if I want to come all the way IFR or would prefer to cancel and fly straight to the airport. The ceiling is okay and the visibility excellent, no sign of the forecast snow showers, so I figure that canceling will expedite things. Approach agrees.

"Okay sir, fly direct Laurel and contact tower now on 119.1."

Laurel?

The area chart has an odd, eye-test cast in the blue-tinged map light, and the thicket of navaids and TCA markings blurs before my eyes. *Laurel*?

"Uh, Kennedy Approach, 48 Quebec back with you. . . . Is that Laurel an intersection?"

"Negative, 48 Quebec; it's the compass outer locater, and the frequency is 226. Tell you what: if you want to cheat a bit, you can just tune the VOR and fly direct to it. That'll take you right over Laurel."

Thank God I'm not solid IFR in snow without an autopilot if

I'm not even ready to find the outer marker. My eyes wander out the side window as we settle into a brief cruise calm, and for a millisecond, I think to myself, "Isn't that interesting: there's now a long black airscoop of some sort on top of the nacelle." A lunge for the flashlight makes it clear that the "airscoop" is actually a wide river of oil streaming back from the oil-fill door atop the nacelle.

Have you ever wondered whether you'd declare The Dreaded Emergency if something like that happened? Don't wonder; you'll declare an emergency. At least I did.

"Kennedy Approach, it's 48 Quebec. I'm losing oil out of my left engine, and I'd like to declare an emergency and request a straight-in."

"That's approved 48 Quebec, squawk 7700 and turn to a heading of 210."

I punch off the autopilot, which I've been fighting with my first rush of adrenaline, and mentally run through the engine-feather procedure. The oil pressure and temperature are rock-steady and normal, however, so I do nothing more than come back on the left engine power. And then I realize that I'm determinedly flying toward an unfamiliar airport 20 miles away with home base 5 or 10 miles behind me. What am I going to do with a single-engine 310 at JFK? We'll all end up taking the limousine home. So I tell Kennedy that maybe I'd better head back to the barn.

"Roger, 48 Quebec, turn to a heading of 350 and descend to 2,000." I obediently do exactly as the controller says, giving up 1,000 feet of altitude that I might just as soon have in the bank if the left engine does quit. "And you can contact Westchester Radar on 126.4. They have the information on you, and the emergency equipment is standing by."

I grind back toward the airport with one eye on the oil-pressure gauge, wondering briefly if I should feather the engine at the beginning of the approach rather than having to shut it down—

or burn it up—on short final if I do lunch the last of the oil, but I quickly terminate the debate as an unnecessary complication and soldier on with everything running.

The crash trucks are primed to chase me down the runway as I roll out, but I spoil their act by making the turnoff at the intersection where they are poised, and we circle, sniffing at each other like mating dogs. I am wondering whether I'm supposed to follow the red station wagon with the flashing light; it is trying to get behind me to see if my vital fluids are indeed spilling out.

And so it ends, on a dark, empty airport, with ground control petulantly asking me to please squawk standby because my code 7700 is still jangling approach's scope. The fire trucks mutter off to their garage, and I am left with my oily airplane.

Why did the oil pour out? Not because the lineman had added a quart and then left the cap off, but because the pilot had done such a lousy preflight that he hadn't caught the mistake. Because he'd left the airplane key home and then let the simple act of retrieving it affect the safety of his flight.

Perhaps one of the few things I did right was to declare an emergency immediately—an act that, despite most authority-resisting airmen's worst fears, got me nothing but instant help and the free use of two crash vehicles. Once I turned off the transponder, the FAA had no further interest in my "emergency."

After all, anybody as careless as I was that night needs all the help he can get.

Whatever else he did, at least our harried pilot had the sense to yell for help. Declaring an emergency can conjure up visions of diabolical questioning by the Feds; but it can also be a very smart move.

Our next pilot faced the wrath of the elements and also, for all we know, that of his wife, with whom he was planning to attend a party this particular evening. But before the party, he had to attend an afternoon business meeting, and his Comanche would allow him to do both. At least, that was the plan.

My duel with adversity began, that Friday afternoon, with a phone call from our office in Banff, Alberta, demanding my presence there. Now Banff is only 160 miles southeast of Jasper, my home, but my wife and I were scheduled to go to a dinner party that evening, so driving was out of the question. Besides, I was a pilot, unfettered by the bonds that hold others to earth-bound means of travel. I had about 100 hours total time, and my newly bought 1959 Comanche, CF-ZPB, could whisk me off to Banff—as well as to my first experience with night flying, ice, the old sucker trap and *get-home-itis*.

Jasper had a high overcast when I topped off at Jasper Airport. Topping the tanks there was the only smart move I made that day. About 1 hour and 15 minutes later, having flown down the outside of the Rocky Mountains, I turned in over Lake Minne-wanka and landed at Banff. A quick run into town, a rush of business, and I was back at he airstrip by 5:30 P.M. Banff was clear and sunny, so I elected to head up the valley along Highway 93 back to Jasper. I'd be home in about an hour, and then we'd be off to the party.

As with many great plans, this one was destined for alteration. As I approached the Columbia Icefields, about 75 miles south of Jasper, the pass was blocked by a snowstorm, and an overcast had obscured the mountaintops. Well, I was a smart pilot, and so I began the 180-degree turn that would get me the hell out of there. Furthermore, there is a nice, wide valley through which the North Saskatchewan River flows on its way east. I'd go out there, get to the outside of the Rockies and head home. The wife would be happy.

The overcast lowered, reducing the clearance between the valley floor and the clouds to about 5,000 feet, which wasn't that bad except that the end of the valley was plugged by a violent electrical storm that I was most reluctant to penetrate. Lightning has a very unnerving effect on me.

Like a puppy, and harboring visions of the wife impatiently tapping her foot as she awaited me, I did a couple of 360s to decide what to do. Brain fade set in as I noticed a small valley running off to the northeast and looking very bright at the far end.

Boy, I thought, here is the way out: go up the valley, skip over to the outside, and home we go. But the bright spot turned dark before I got to it, and the overcast was blocking the way out. Another 180 and—whoops!—the thunderstorm had moved up the Saskatchewan Valley. There was nothing left to do now; I had to go into it.

Immediately, I ran out of VFR and turned another 180 to exit the blackness back to my little bright-spot valley. There I was, making ovals about 25 miles long and 3 miles wide in a socked-in valley, with rocks to the right of me, rocks to the left of me, rocks in front of me, a thunderstorm behind me, cloud above me and bush below. No sweat yet, though. My brain power seemed full on.

As I had left Banff heading northward, the overcast had appeared to top out at about 12,000 or 13,000 feet. Rather than go left, right, forward, back or down, I decided to go up through the clouds, break out, turn south, find a hole, descend, and head home. I had just completed, about two weeks before, 2.5 hours of instrument training. I'd had no problems and had even been complimented by the instructor on my abilities. Was I not Superpilot?

Full of confidence, I climbed to the bottom of the overcast, leveled at 6,000 and flew the length of the valley once more, to make sure of my compass headings. At the end of the valley, I took the heading, put on full power and pointed the airplane upward. There was turbulence, which made it extremely difficult to hold my heading. I dropped a wing a couple of times but finally approached 12,000 feet. I was still in the soup, so I climbed some more. At 14,000, I looked out of the windows and couldn't see a thing, not even the wings. Pucker time.

And the airplane was covered with ice.

It was my first experience with the stuff, and I had no idea how much I had taken on or how long my steed would continue to fly. The real gravity of the situation was apparent. I was in trouble, real bare-bones, luck-out trouble. The only alternative was to turn eastward and hope that when old ZPB decided to stop flying, there would be flat land and warm air below. I headed east, about 065 degrees, maintained altitude for twenty minutes and then went down.

The turbulence was worse, and I again had trouble with my heading—even dropping into a spiral a couple of times. I had visions of the wreckage of ZPB scattered among the rocks and trees below. Yet once I faced the realization that I was looking at very short odds for my survival, I became calm and relaxed. Fear disappeared. And I was truly alone. My radio was on my mantelpiece at home, awaiting a new tube.

The duel was joined. Many of the clouds around me had very hard centers. Cumulo-granite. But after another twenty minutes, I trimmed back to 100 mph and started down again. Then the engine quit. A quick check revealed that a tank had gone empty. A rapid switchover, and the power returned.

The ice came off at just under 10,000 feet, and I broke out of the clouds at just under 9,000, over rolling foothills. Which foothills I knew not, but I turned north, hopefully toward Jasper.

Now, the final irony. It was beginning to get dark, and there were no lighted runways within 200 miles, but I had a choice of several strips. I could now tell that I was approaching Hinton, but soon it was dark, and then it started to rain heavily. Over the airport, I could see straight down but had no lateral visibility. I headed for Jasper and found the same thing, so I headed back to Hinton, with less than an hour of fuel left. I buzzed the town several times before someone got the idea, and soon the runway was lit by cars; I made my first night landing.

Short flights can teach you more than long ones sometimes, and this one was full of lessons. I had trusted the weather and my own prowess as a pilot too much, so determined was I to hurry home. Bit by bit, I pushed the limits of my knowledge and experience until sheer luck became the key ingredient of my survival—that, and the last-minute help of my neighbors. All that rushing and dueling with hazard was for naught. We still missed the party.

All of which must have left this pilot wondering whether the overwhelming desire to get home, to prove the usefulness of the newly acquired airplane, to please the wife, to attend a mere party was worth the occasional terror he must have felt at various stages of the flight.

It's in the course of keeping the boss pleased, too, that pilots can find themselves in a sky they would prefer to have left for others to explore. The pressures on a charter or air-taxi pilot to fly can be greater than his sense of his own capabilities. But if he is to keep his job, he has to keep the boss content, so he has to fly, whether he wants to or not. This pilot didn't want to, especially after he'd shut down one engine of the Twin Beech on a snowy night over Pittsburgh.

The massive storm that will turn out to be the first of the blizzards of '78 is inbound from the Midwest, and temperatures are already in the low teens. The Twin Beech has been sitting out in the cold for a month now, while another pilot and I alternate weeks in Pittsburgh running freight back and forth to Philadelphia.

As a result of the sudden drop in temperature and my inexperience with the Wasp Juniors, the Tuesday night run is canceled. I call my boss and tell him both starters are shot, but he insists it's just the cold. It occurs to me that he's 200 miles away and has no idea what it's like out here, but I follow his advice, and next afternoon try again with heat and an auxiliary power unit.

The starters are definitely shot. That cancels Wednesday night as well, and the pressure rises. My boss arrives early on Thursday with a mechanic and two starters. By one o'clock, the engines are running. I return to the motel to get some sleep for the flight tonight; they go back home.

While I sleep, snow rolls into the area. Some Indiana and Ohio airports are already closed. I go out to the airport early, knowing that PIT will probably be closed by the time I'm scheduled to leave for Philadelphia. So far, I'm not too worried, but I can't ignore the two previous cancellations.

When I get to the airport at 10:00, the snow has been falling heavily for some time. Big, white flakes driven by a 15-knot wind have created large drifts everywhere, and the linemen ask whether I'll go tonight. I avoid giving them a direct answer.

It's time to check the latest sequences in hopes that the visibility has gone below departure minimums or that they've closed the airport. No such luck. In fact, the runway visual range is a good 3,000 feet more than I need. I've already preflighted the airplane. All that's left is to pick up the cargo, return to get the snow removed, then make a final weather check.

By the time the engines are running, the windshield is again opaque with snow. I don't care if we did cancel the last two nights; I can't even taxi. I shut down the engines and go into the FBO to call the boss. As I dial the number and hear the distant ringing down the wires, the tension builds.

"It's me again. The snow's falling pretty hard out here, and it looks like the airport's going to close before the night's out. I just tried to taxi out of the ramp over to cargo and I could hardly see."

The reply is markedly more calm and confident than my own voice. "What's the RVR?"

"Actually, it's better than 4,500."

"Then it's legal to go, isn't it?"

"Yes," I said.

"We've canceled two nights this week already, and things are pretty tight."

"Okay, I'll do my best."

For the second time, I crank up the R-985s. The electric blue flames from the exhaust stacks provide a brilliant contrast to the ominous snow-covered masses around me—airplanes, trucks, buildings. Outside the cockpit, artificial light reflects off the snowflakes still rapidly falling. It seems that almost everyone else has canceled. The ramp at cargo is usually alive with people and airplanes, loading and unloading. Tonight, I seem to be the only one moving.

I make one last check of the weather as the snow is melted off the plane with alcohol sprayed from an old, broken-down truck. The lineman leads me out of the ramp area and I notice that my old tracks have already been wiped out. As I run up into a gusting 40-degree crosswind, I begin to slide across the snow. I call for a last check on the RVR. Except for a slight tendency to slide across the runway, the takeoff is uneventful; I am relieved as I clean up and climb.

I begin to feel comfortable. The Beech and I are good friends; I can almost set the power by the sound of the engines and the feel of the spread between the throttles. No structural ice is forming, and I begin to laugh at my nervousness.

The right manifold pressure seems to be lagging a little. That needle has always stuck some in the cold, but I throw some manifold heat onto it anyway. I wish the carburetor heat box were a little tighter; seems like the carburetor air temperature isn't as high as it should be.

I overhear center tell an inbound that PIT is now closed. That manifold pressure on the right side is too low, and the throttle is already against the limit. The manifold heat isn't doing anything.

"Center, I'm unable to maintain 9,000, requesting 7,000."

"Roger, maintain 7,000 and advise your situation."

Now I'm really busy. The manifold pressure is falling off rapidly, and I'm going to have to feather. Thank God I'm carrying only a little freight. I advise center that I am unable to maintain 7,000 and have just feathered the right engine.

I've got to make a decision. I'm losing 500 feet per minute and heading into some high terrain. I get the engine secured but have to use both feet on the left rudder. My knees are shaking. I'm through 6,000 and still descending. Center again requests my intentions. When I tell him that I think I can make it to Harrisburg, he hints that my terrain and altitude are not compatible and asks if I want to return to PIT, or go into Johnstown or Latrobe, which are also below minimums. I elect to return to PIT and declare an emergency. My altitude stabilizes at 4,000, with a disconcertingly slow airspeed in moderate to heavy turbulence. PIT is still officially closed, and the headwind will make these the most agonizing 60 miles of my life.

Just as things seem to settle down, I notice that the left oil temperature is fluctuating wildly; I reduce power as much as I dare in case the engine is overheating. My heart starts to beat like a drum. For the first time I start to pray. Luckily, it appears that the instrument just happened to go haywire at that moment, and the engine continues to run smoothly.

Center hands me off to PIT after I join the localizer. He wishes me luck and I thank him, hoping he knows how grateful I am for his help. From time to time a downdraft catches me and I run up to METO power to maintain the little altitude I have. In fifteen minutes, I have asked for my range from the airport about five times.

I'm holding my own, adjusting to a skewed attitude gyro that requires a 5-degree bank to maintain a heading. Approach prods me to stay on course. Concentrate, concentrate. Finally, the glide-slope begins to drop toward the doughnut. The controller asks if I want to stay with him or go over to the tower. He's my good-luck charm, and I don't want him to go; he clears me to land.

When I break out, I see a runway covered with snow. At least the crosswind is on the side of the good engine. Moments later, I'm down and inwardly exploding with joy. Shortly after I land, another Twin Beech comes in on one engine. Two in one night and we're both alive. I meet him later in the lounge; we swap stories and let off steam.

Now comes the time to call the boss. We didn't make it again tonight, but at least he still has a plane and a pilot. For me, there's plenty of time to reflect on who makes the final decision to go.

Of all the lessons the pilot learned, the most important one was that he *was pilot in command. He—not his boss, who was probably curled up cozily with a book and a coffee—was the person who would have to taxi blind in driving snow and head for an airport that in all probability would be closed before he arrived. But the pressure to fly was heavy: he had canceled the two previous nights' trips.*

Here's a pair of pilots in a hurry to get to Washington in an Islander. Each pilot thought the other had finished the preflight, until that moment came when they looked at each other, as if to say, "I didn't; did you?"

I was a young instructor working for a young company that was rapidly expanding into all areas of general aviation. Having started instructing with the company just a few months before, I was already flying single-engine charter and beginning to check out on the twins as a copilot.

This particular day, a cold and overcast one, I had been off on a single-engine charter. Entering downwind, I spotted our new Britten-Norman Islander on its tie-down and smiled to myself because I knew I might get to go as copilot on a charter from Washington National to Ocean City that afternoon.

The chief pilot was on the phone as I walked into the office. He motioned me in and told me to preflight the Islander; we had to be in Washington in thirty minutes. He didn't have to tell me twice. I sped out to the ramp. There were to be two deadhead legs on this trip, and that meant I would get to fly left seat to Washington and back home from Ocean City.

I started the preflight by opening the cockpit door and flipping up the master switch to check the fuel level. Then I took a short stepladder and carefully checked the left engine compartment for bird nests, before moving around to the left side of the cowling to check the oil and the fuel cap. I got down from the ladder and started toward the left wingtip, hauling the ladder with me, as I would need it for the tail section and the other engine. Just then our secretary called from the office door. I had a telephone call, and this particular student had been trying to reach me all day.

I laid the ladder down and ran to the phone. The chief pilot headed out the door, obviously in a hurry. As we passed, he told me to make it quick; we were already late. I finished scheduling the student and rushed back to the ramp, to find the chief waiting impatiently in the right seat with the right engine running. Having jumped in the left seat and fired up the other engine, I was preparing to move away from the chocks when the chief said he wanted to show me how to taxi without using the brakes. "Now look, we'll keep both feet flat on the floor and use nothing but the throttles."

The Islander has a castoring nosewheel, and we had been replacing brakes about every forty hours, an unacceptably frequent maintenance job. As we broke away from the chocks, the chief skillfully made the hard turn out to the taxiway, then another hard left onto the uphill taxiway toward Runway 14. As we headed up the slope he lectured me on using the brakes unnecessarily; we would all have to learn to use differential power to taxi. The chief cycled both props, and I reached up and checked both mags at the same time. Neither one of us had touched the flight controls yet.

The chief swung onto the runway using differential power, pushed the throttles forward and told me I had it. If you are unfamiliar with the Islander, you must understand a little about it to comprehend what happened next. The Islander is a true STOL aircraft. With two people on board, half fuel and a 10- to 15-knot wind, its short-field ability is awesome—keeping it on the ground for 300 or 400 feet would require a conscious effort.

As the airplane accelerated, we began to drift to the left. Nothing happened when I instinctively pressed hard right rudder. The chief grabbed the yoke, yelling at me to get off the controls. In an instant we were airborne and climbing at an extremely high deck angle. I still did not know what was happening, but then I heard the chief scream, "My God, the gust locks! We forgot the damn gust locks!" The realization of those words crushed me with a force I have never felt before—shock, fear, anger, the whole spectrum of human emotions in the wink of an eye.

As we headed nearly straight up, I made my sole constructive move in this whole incident by grabbing the throttles and pulling the power off. As the nose fell through level-flight attitude I shoved the power forward, and in a second or two we had the power set for our trim condition.

The chief then took control of the throttles and, using differential power, made a very shallow teardrop turn. I remember saying that our best shot would be to land straight ahead. The chief disagreed—he was going to get us back to the airport if he could. After completing the turn, which took four or five miles, we were lined up on Runway 32 with about 500 feet of altitude. The chief then began to reduce power, while turning the trim wheel forward, as if to trim the nose down (the trim works in reverse when the elevator is locked). Easing the power off over the runway, we made a hard but damage-free three-point landing and rolled to a stop. I looked over at the chief. His head was resting on his arm over the yoke, but he aroused himself to reach up and pull the mixture.

Having sat in silence for a while, we swore never to tell anyone about the episode. But that was many years ago. The shock and shame have worn away, and maybe someone else will learn a lesson from it, the way I did.

We were late, and the Islander was a simple airplane, just a big twin-engine Cub with fixed gear. We took its simplicity for granted. The chief took it for granted that I had completed the preflight, and I took it for granted that he had. We learned one more lesson, too: never give up.

Apart from the obvious lessons of preflighting properly, the incident showed the two pilots that, however dismal the situation, it never pays to give up the fight as lost. Fortunately, they were on board a relatively docile airplane, but they will probably never again be fooled into seeing it as just a big twin-engine Cub.

Here's a tale of an airplane that, by rights, shouldn't have flown because of an oversight by the tired and eager-to-be-home pilot. But fly it did, if in a precarious and unpredictable manner.

Was it my fifth flight of the day, or the sixth? It didn't matter. The only thing that mattered was that I was tired and not paying attention. I was flying a Cessna Cardinal RG to one of the few paved Indian reservation strips in Arizona—most are dirt—to pick up two accountants, and I had been sitting bleary-eyed in my seat for over an hour, half-watching the world slide beneath the wings and wishing I were elsewhere. Descending, I methodically ran through the prelanding checklist and waited for the familiar runway to reveal itself from behind the canyon wall east of the field. As the airport finally peeked over the rim, I added the last of the flaps and verified that the landing gear was down and locked.

The approach was routine, a hard right turn, throttle pulled back to idle, and the little Cessna gliding toward the runway numbers. I took a final glance at the airspeed, tugged gently on the yoke and was rewarded with two quick chirps as the main-wheels touched asphalt. I taxied to the terminal and shut down the engine to await my passengers' arrival. The vigil in the one-room terminal building seemed endless, and the afternoon Arizona heat was draining. The sound of an approaching car was welcome relief: my passengers had arrived.

They parked the big Ford next to the tail of the airplane and bade me a clipped "hello"; we began transferring a week's worth of baggage from the trunk of the car to the aft compartment of the aircraft. That done, I settled into my seat, half-dozing while my passengers stood on the ramp in their three-piece suits exchanging pleasantries with the driver of the car. The two accountants, with their attaché cases, seemed noticeably out of place against the backdrop of tumbleweeds and rocks.

At last the men boarded, one of them in back and the other beside me to offset the weight of the baggage in the aft section. I started the engine and enjoyed the rush of air from the prop through the open cabin doors. There were two muffled thuds as I reluctantly closed them down, then another sharper noise as the driver of the Ford rapped on the fuselage: a startling way to say good-bye, I thought.

We taxied toward the runway, and I mechanically ran down the checklist, performing the ritual movements as I read. "Cabin doors closed and locked, fuel selector on both, flight controls free and correct," and on and on.

I snaked the Cessna onto the runway, pushed the throttle home, and we rolled toward takeoff. I waited until the airspeed needle crept past 52 knots and then pulled gently on the control wheel to urge the airplane skyward. Nothing happened. ''No problem,'' I thought. It was hot outside. I waited for another 4 knots to register and pulled again. Nothing happened. ''We're heavy,'' I thought. The runway was beginning to diminish noticeably in length as the airspeed needle inched past 61. I pulled once more at the yoke and still the airplane had no desire to leave the ground. Were we that heavy?

It was now too late to abort the takeoff. I reached over and swatted the flap lever to the 10-degree position in the hope of gaining some additional lift, and then pulled harder on the yoke. The airplane staggered into the air with barely 50 yards of asphalt remaining. Something was very wrong. The control wheel jerked spasmodically back and forth in my hand, and the whole airplane twitched like a wounded animal. The last inches of runway zipped beneath, and the airspeed needle crawled to 70 and stopped. Only feet above the earth, the Cessna ceased to climb.

I gripped the control wheel with both hands to dampen the shaking, by now violent, as we pitched along, almost dragging the sagebrush. What the heck was wrong with the airplane? Although we badly needed to climb, I dared not retract the flaps or landing gear for fear of further disturbing the airflow over the stricken machine.

The terrain sloped downhill just ahead, and we had 50 feet of air beneath us. I stole a quick glance at the tail and froze in disbelief. There, wrapped around the left side of the stabilator, were two garment bags, each containing a trio of three-piece suits belonging to my passengers. I was amazed we were in the air at all with only half a tail—not to mention the fact that the sheer weight of the bags so far back was ruining our balance.

The accountants turned around and saw the bags. They laughed, then admonished me not to drop them! I told them that we would return to the field and ''onload them with the rest of the baggage.'' It seemed a bad time to expound on my own opinion that we would never make it back to the airport; that the airplane seemed determined to shake off its tail, or failing that, to fly us into the ground for want of proper control response or horsepower or both. Some things are better left unsaid.

I began a shallow turn back toward the field. The airplane wallowed and shuddered and threatened to fall out of the sky. The turn took forever. My accountants were silent now, but still unafraid because they didn't understand.

The runway beckoned ahead and to the right, a mile or so distant, up a gentle slope that might just as well have been a mountain. The airplane continued to shake madly and still refused to climb, until a column of hot desert air tossed it another 50 feet aloft. We would make the runway. We crossed the threshold, still doing 70 knots, with the wheels skimming the sagebrush. I pulled the throttle an inch from the firewall. The tires smacked the pavement and we rolled to a stop.

Back at the terminal, the man in the Ford was still standing there, awaiting our return. "Hey, I found these on the backseat of the car," he said, pointing to the bags, which were still draped over the tail. "So I threw them on the tail and banged on your airplane with my fist to get you to stop. But you just kept on going. Hey, lucky they didn't fall off, huh?"

"Yeah, lucky they didn't," I echoed.

One of my passengers, a regular charter customer, interrupted. "Didn't you feel them when you checked the controls?"

"No," I said, which was the truth. "They weren't tangled up in anything; they were just lying over the tail. Next time I'll look out the back window." Which was also the truth.

What must have made this pilot feel even more of a klutz was how visible his external cargo would have been, if only he'd been alert and patient enough to look for it. In the next confession, the gremlin was a sinister one hidden away inside the skin of the

Cessna 310—but no less visible if the pilots had cared to look for it. The airplane had just come out of maintenance, and the pilots omitted one vital pretakeoff check: controls full and free and correct.

"I need a biennial review," he said. "Mine has expired and I need to fly down to Arkansas tonight."

It was four in the afternoon and I always tried to leave work by five on Fridays, so this gave an additional sense of urgency to the matter. The pilot was an old friend I had known since he had attended our flight school many years before. The airplane was a 310 that had just come out of a maintenance shop after an annual inspection. Our flight was to be a combination test flight and biennial review. I watched him drain the fuel sumps and complete the line inspection. "Everything is fine," he said, "shall we give it a try?"

We climbed in, started up, and he called ground control but had some difficulty establishing contact. They kept saying they couldn't hear him very well, but we finally managed to get clearance to the end of Runway 24, which is 4,100 feet long.

After run-up, which revealed no problems, he switched to the tower and again had difficulty making radio contact. The controller finally said if we'd turn toward the tower, he would flash us a light. It was a bad omen. I didn't want to take off with a faulty radio; there were many thunderstorms in the area and I thought we might want to return quickly, without having to circle the airport for a green light.

On a hunch, I reached down and pulled the microphone plug from the jack and discovered it was green with corrosion. I scratched most of it off with my fingernail and plugged it back in. On the next transmission, the tower controller said we were coming in loud and clear.

I watched while the pilot started the takeoff roll. We accelerated almost to Vmc and then suddenly the pilot pulled back both throttles and braked to a stop. "I had to shut down," he said. "There seems to be something wrong with the trim."

I looked at the tab indicators. They all were in neutral position. I opened the cabin door and looked at the rudder tab. It also was in neutral position.

"What does it feel like?" I asked.

"It wants to go left even with full right rudder," he replied.

Well, as complacent people will do, we taxied back to try another takeoff run. We should have gone back to the shop, shut down and taken a better look at everything, but the pilot had to go to Arkansas that evening and I had to go home early. We got in position for the second takeoff roll. I noticed that the pilot had the control wheel in the neutral position; because the wind was across the runway from the right, I reached up and turned the wheel full right to correct for the crosswind. If this is going to be a biennial review, I thought, I might as well correct errors in pilot technique. This was the only action I took before the takeoff run, and I believe it probably saved our lives.

As our roll started, I monitored the power because I suspected a partial power loss on the left engine as the cause of the airplane's left-turning tendency. We reached liftoff speed and he began to pull up the nose. The airplane immediately rolled to the left. By this time we seemed only 10 or 12 feet above the runway. We continued to roll left, even though the pilot held the wheel full right, until the left tip tank hit the runway. Then the wheels left the ground, leaving only that tip tank sliding along the pavement at 100 mph.

Suddenly, I thought that this was the end of everything for me. I was certain the airplane would complete the roll and end up on its back.

We slid along for at least 100 yards until the pilot pulled both throttles back to idle. The airplane came back on its wheels but headed off the runway. It seemed we weren't going to stop before we met either a large hangar or a DC-3 parked in front of it, and I remembered something about emergency procedures from the Beech D18s that I used to fly. It wouldn't work in 310s at all, but I yelled, "Raise the gear!"

The gear on a 310 has a safety switch that prevents retraction on the ground. All we achieved by putting the gear lever in the "up" position was an intermittent wailing of the gear horn as we bounced over the rough sod between the runway and the taxiway. The old Beech I used to fly had disabling switches to retract the gear when you were headed for the boondocks and didn't have enough brake to stop. The Beech gear also retracted backward, with no nosewheel to complicate things, so you could slide gracefully to a stop on the protruding main wheels. I am glad the wheels didn't come up on that 310; we would have bent both props, warped the engine mounts, possibly damaged both crankshafts, and maybe both crankcases and, last but not least, probably damaged both wing spars.

Somehow we missed the hangar and the DC-3, coming to a halt about 200 feet from the airport boundary. We sat there for a few seconds, relishing the fact that we were in one piece—except for the tip tank, which was gushing fuel.

After the fire and rescue equipment arrived, I was standing there—still in something of a daze—when I realized why the whole incident had occurred. I climbed back on the wing, reached in through the door, and turned the control wheel. You may have guessed already: the ailerons were rigged in reverse.

I won't go into detail about my thoughts . . . what could have happened if the airplane had gotten high enough to roll inverted, or what if there had been an airplane on the taxiway we had crossed at high speed after our wheels had come down to the runway again. My instinctive action to roll the control wheel full right against the crosswind was certainly timely; if we had taken off with the control wheel in neutral, the airplane probably would have climbed high enough to roll inverted.

I'll never again believe that the odds against aileron cables' getting reversed in the shop are so great that I can ignore them. Will I ever become complcent again? Perhaps, but I hope it takes another 15,000 hours.

It was not quite the sort of takeoff roll they had been expecting. Checklists might be time-consuming, but they can spot surprises before they're real surprises.

In the next case of haste nearly making waste, the pilot was determined to make his transcontinental solo flight in one day—even if it meant skimping on the preflight at a fuel stop. He'd missed something important, but he didn't know it until it was too late.

As I dressed in the predawn light on that June 21, the thought recurred. "It really is a long flight, and at least two days, possibly more, should be allowed for it." But adventurousness made me want to try flying from Washington's Dulles Airport to San Diego's Montgomery Field in one day. The equipment for this solo flight was a B model Debonair. The prevailing winds would work against me, but the three-hour time difference would present a daylight bonus.

A call to flight service assured me that I would receive plenty of instrument training that day, as a weak cold front and scattered thunderstorms lay across much of my projected path. Just after dawn, feeling lonely but confident, I climbed through a thin overcast and began a turn to the west. This first four-hour leg would terminate with a refueling stop at a field in Illinois. Having spent the last two hours of the leg staring at the gauges, I was only too happy to execute a VOR approach to minimums and land. The airport was very quiet, but it provided a friendly shelter on that rainy first day of summer.

The FBO, who was also the lineman, refueled the Debonair and checked the oil, while I enjoyed a Coke and made a pit stop of my own. A long-distance call to St. Louis Center resulted in a clearance to Oklahoma City. I had to report airborne in ten minutes, or the clearance would be void.

The preflight! How many of us are most careful in the preflight for the first time round but ever more casual for each successive flight of the day? After all, we have just flown the darn thing, so what could possibly be wrong? With my clearance limit of ten minutes in mind, I paid the FBO, quickly checked that the tanks were full, looked under the cowling—wait! No, everything seemed okay there—then scanned the outside of the airplane. I fired up and taxied smartly to the threshold—no need to worry about the traffic that day. Eight minutes had elapsed since my call, but with a long instrument flight in the offing, it seemed prudent to check the mags. All the dials looked good, so with a smooth push on the throttle, I was launched on leg number two.

By the time the airplane had been cleaned up for a comfortable cruise-climb, ten minutes had elapsed since my phone call to center. I pressed the microphone button: ''St. Louis Center, this is Debonair—Good God! The windshield is covered with oil. I'm declaring an emergency and returning to the field.'' The clouds were just above me, so I pushed the nose down and set the throttle to low cruise power. Although the engine instruments showed no symptoms, a 180-degree turn to the field and a prompt landing seemed wise. Even with gear and flaps down, I was unable to bleed off enough speed and altitude to land downwind, so with application of power, I crossed the length of the field at an altitude of 200 feet. Once more I turned to land, now able to see only through the side panel, but I was still too high, and again I could not land. Another quick glance at the panel informed me that the engine, so far at least, was doing just fine. With a slowly returning feeling of confidence, I decided to fly a normal pattern. On this third attempt, the trusty Debonair touched down.

Meeting the plane at the gas pumps were the FBO and his wife. They were quite concerned about my flying antics, and St. Louis Center had politely inquired as to my health. The problem was immediately apparent: the oil dipstick was lying on the fuel pump. Had the dipstick only been loose, or something, my hurried preflight might have sufficed. The engine required a quart of oil, which was kindly donated by the FBO.

My second request to center resulted in the same clearance, except this time the kind gentleman suggested that it would not be necessary for me to report airborn within ten minutes. It would be quite all right if I took my time. I performed a much more careful preflight—as I do now before *every* flight. While the FBO felt bad about my experience, the true responsibility was, of course, my own. Oh, yes, sundown saw me happily back on course at San Diego after sixteen hours at the controls.

5

There Are Limits

Aviation is a potentially risky pursuit, so its practitioners are made to be keenly aware of the limitations that are imposed on man and machine, and on the way man operates that machine. The idea behind the limits, of course, is to reduce any risks to the absolute minimum humanly possible. Trouble is, to reduce that risk to zero, it would be necessary to remove the human element completely, and that would mean no aviation. The human element is usually the one to disregard the limits: for example, airframes don't decide to overstress themselves and shed components.

As can be seen in most of the stories in this book, it is the pilot who launches himself into his predicament, and sometimes that predicament takes the airplane beyond the envelope for which it was designed. More often than not, the pilot exceeds his own limitations and takes his airplane with him.

In the first tale of jousting with limits in this chapter, a passenger—not the pilot—is telling the story. He is telling it because he, too, is a pilot, but on this occasion he could only sit in the back and watch in terror as the occupant of the left seat took the airplane farther and farther below minimums on a non-precision instrument approach in fog.

I've flown a lot of different airplanes in a lot of different flight conditions, but today I am a passenger in a corporate King Air with two full-time pilots up front. And I am absolutely petrified. Why? Because the minimums on the ADF approach we're flying are 800 and 2, and the airplane is solid IFR 300 feet above the ground. Four things occupy my mind: two water towers, a smokestack and a power line.

What, I wonder, am I doing here, and why is a conservative, AAA-rated *Fortune* 500 company operating an airplane in this manner?

Our company's headquarters are in Atlanta, Georgia, with

divisions and plants all over the country. I'm accompanying a group of customers from Minneapolis, Minnesota, to one of our plants. The weather is good on departure, but scattered clouds gradually develop into a solid undercast. Although I enjoy flying my own Bonanza, I'm glad someone else is flying today so that I can devote my attention to business.

The weather reporting station nearest our plant is a large ILS-equipped field about 50 miles away. Our pilot calls for weather and receives a report of 300 overcast, three-quarters of a mile with drizzle and fog. A few miles further on, he calls unicom at our destination and receives an informal zero/zero report from the airport operator, who says he can't even see the other side of the airport parking lot. I suggest that we go directly to the ILS airport in order to arrive at the plant no later than necessary, but the pilot replies, "You don't know about an approach until you try it." He's right, and anyway, he's the captain. I twist in my seat so that I can watch the action.

Beacon inbound, my attention is riveted on the panel. With a heading of 282 and the ADF needle 10 degrees to the right of due aft, our pilot tracks 272 degrees toward the airport in a northeast wind. The copilot keeps track of time, and we descend steadily, the PT6s humming reassuringly. The cockpit becomes dark, and a combination of rain and snow begins to splatter the windshield as we near 800 feet—minimums.

Two minutes to go, and the King Air slides right through 800 feet, the view out front is still dark, wet and featureless. The pilot's expression is determined, as if he can will the airport into place in front of us. As we go through 600 feet agl, I fight the urge to say something, feeling that it might just make a bad situation even worse. At 300 agl, my concern becomes real tension. An occasional ghostlike tree zips by in the fog, and I know that somewhere nearby, a water tower is moving steadily toward us at a relative velocity of 120 knots.

We pass the vague outline of a barn. The copilot sees it and tells the pilot to turn left. About 100 feet above the trees, he gets another cue from a barely visible blur that I judge to be a 10,000-volt power line, turns farther left and suddenly comes upon the runway at a right angle to our heading. A hard right turn, full flaps, power all the way back and we are lined up. "How much runway we got left?" the pilot asks. "Plenty," the copilot says. Perhaps he has recognized something, perhaps he simply wants to get down. We land and brake hard, the props yowling in reverse, and the King Air turns off the 5,000-foot runway. We have yet to see either end of the strip.

One passenger lingers for a word with the pilots. He compliments them, saying it must be hard to land when you can't see and tells our captain he'd fly anywhere with him—he was that impressed.

As my blood pressure slowly drops, my fury about this aeronautical insanity grows. I call the division vice-president who is in charge of our flight department to ask what kind of operation he thinks he's running. Super, he replies—passengers are carried, schedules are met, courtesy abounds and inconveniences are almost unknown. The pilots, he says, are excellent. Excellent, I inquire? Decidedly so, he replies; they have lots of time in company airplanes over company routes, and they know the airports near our plants better than anyone in the world. He volunteers a comparison between company operations and charters, which he considers unreliable—perhaps even unsafe. On a recent IFR charter flight, he says, the pilot missed the approach at the airport where I had just landed and had to shoot an ILS 50 miles away. That wouldn't happen with our crew.

It doesn't take long for me to arrange a high-level meeting on flying safety. Trusting veteran passengers are amazed as Jeppesen charts are projected on a screen and the concept of minimum descent altitude is explained. A strict policy of adherence to published procedures develops, and a fleet of station wagons is procured to provide transport from low-minimums airports to our plants in poor weather.

Trying to please a passenger is a lousy reason for descending below minimums. Trying to impress your boss is an even worse excuse.

Instrument flying is a religion that uses a brown loose-leaf binder as a bible, and whose participants must be orthodox if they (and the passengers they carry) are to survive. To disregard the tablets of stone is to court disaster.

In the next duel with adversity, the pilot discovers there are limits to how much a Cherokee 140 will lift off an uphill runway high above sea level on a hot day.

Surface winds are 9 miles per hour, straight down the 11,500-foot runway. A piece of cake. Sure, the airport elevation is 6,200 feet and the temperature 62° F., but when your home field is a 2,500-foot dirt strip tucked 4,600 feet up an Arizona mountainside, you reach an understanding with density altitude. Or so I thought.

The procedure was familiar: lean the fuel mixture on the run-up pad at full power; pull two notches of flaps; ease the throttle to the wall and begin rotation at 55 mph. At lift-off, release back yoke pressure and accelerate to 74 indicated. Climb out at that speed until the rocks, mesquite and cat claw bushes are cleared. Doing it by the numbers always worked. Except this time.

We rotate nicely after a 2,000-foot ground run. Accelerating just above the runway, I nudge the yoke back at the appointed airspeed. Nothing happens. The airspeed bleeds off and my wife nervously eyes the flickering red stall light. We must have hit a light wind shear or a downdraft—typical mountain stuff. I release back yoke pressure and we again accelerate to the best angle-of-climb speed. There's nothing to worry about yet; this has happened before at higher density altitudes than this. As I lift the nose once again, the response is positive. Fifty, then 70 feet of altitude are gained, slowly as usual in high country.

But my intuition tells me that all is not well; subtle clues begin soaking in slowly. The runway slopes upward gently, but increasingly so, it seems. Either it's coming up or we're going down. We may end up with very little terrain clearance this time. Correction—we will have *no* terrain clearance. My throat tightens.

How does one abort a takeoff? I've never had to do that before, but I know I've got to put it down somewhere. At this point we'll surely roll off the end of the runway, tangling with some pipes and other debris there. I can see that the hill ahead is even worse, crowned with trees and a water tank.

Turn? Can't even think about it; I'm too low and slow. I don't want to hit a tree so, cheating a little, I release right rudder. Our Cherokee 140 obediently drifts toward the smaller hill on the left. The airspeed is dropping: I lower the nose, watching the terrain for height clues. This flight is about to terminate whether I'm ready or not.

The buck stops on a grassy knoll one-third of a mile from the end of the runway. We land firmly as I stand on the brakes, taking out a barbed-wire fence here, hitting the far side of a shallow drainage ditch there. The ELT wails through the cabin speaker. My niece plucks a flying, empty picnic jug out of the air. We lurch to a stop in a cloud of dust 400 feet down the hill. For a second we stare at the white frame house a stone's throw ahead of us, and then we scramble out on shaky legs to sit on the ground out of harm's way. My wife rubs her bruised knee, our niece still holds the picnic jug and our nine-year-old son asks when it will explode.

Terrible guilt creeps in: what have I done?

Our proud little airplane has its prop twisted and its face in the dirt because the nosegear collapsed. Then it hits me. I walk over and remove the fuel-tank caps, and gasoline pours out onto the wings. Both tanks are brimful; an extra 84 pounds I didn't mean to have on board. Sure, I had told the lineman to fill it only to the tabs. ("You mean to the lip under the filler neck?" "No, to the bottom of that metal strip hanging down in there.") His quizzical expression only gains significance now—I never checked his actions. And since my preflight was completed earlier, I whipped out the MasterCard, signed the bill without reading it and piled everyone inside.

The GADO investigator is very understanding and well mannered as I confess our overgross condition, but he still picks and probes. We cover everything: my Cherokee's spark plugs get fouled on every extended trip out of 80-octane Arizona into 100LL territory, the engine has over 2,000 hours on it, our weight was up to maximum allowable gross weight even without excess fuel; the density altitude was about 8,000 feet. Each of these contributed its share.

Out of all these factors, though, the load would have been easiest to control. My failure to check fuel levels resulted in our carrying extra weight that was roughly equivalent to that of a young teenager. I should have been especially conscious of the airplane's loading under those high density-altitude conditions. At least then I would have had a little room for error, rather than playing it all so close to the wire that a minor mistake caused an accident.

I certainly owe my passengers, myself and my airplane a margin of safety at all times. Perhaps 84 pounds would have made the difference that day.

Takeoff weight is the easiest variable to control; you're stuck with everything else—temperature, elevation, runway slope, wind (or lack of it) and the number of horsepower under the cowling. Baggage and fuel, though, can all be juggled to stay within limits.

In the next tale, a crew plumbs the lower limits of competency in a Skyvan over Alaska that loses first one engine, then the second. And nobody seems to be able to unfeather the props for a restart.

I remember very well that cool damp day in August. The Skyvan was heavily loaded with cargo. The fuel tanks were full. We had left Campbell Airstrip in Anchorage early in the morning, flying IFR along Green-9 over the Alaska Range. Our destination was Bethel, Alaska. Our climb-out was slow because of our weight, and our groundspeed was slow because of high southwest winds. Light rime ice slowed our progress even more.

I was bored. It wasn't my leg to fly, and the prospect of Bethel did not excite me. I was contemplating a change in jobs; there was no chance I'd ever be upgraded to captain in the 'van. The hours were long and unpredictable, the pay was inadequate. I considered myself more of a stevedore than a pilot; I could sense that my proficiency was slipping because of my indifference.

Momentarily, we came out of the clouds. A few minutes later we were IFR again. I noticed ice on the air scoops. The inlet-air heaters were off. I asked myself, "Why did he turn them off?" Looking at the captain, I answered my own question: "For a little extra power. We'll be over the mountains in 20 minutes; the ice on the smiles isn't building rapidly. Anyway, it's too late to turn the heaters on now."

I began looking for my World Aeronautical Chart at 55 DME. I wanted to know our exact position so I could give the captain a terrain-clearance heading in case we had a powerplant failure over Merrill Pass. I was still bored; there wasn't anything else to do.

The airplane shuddered. I scanned the instruments: all normal. I noticed the ice was gone from the right inlet scoop. I looked at the captain. "Probably water through the engine," he said. I said, "At least it's still running." I glanced to my left to see that only the right inlet-air heater light was on. I returned to my search for a WAC.

My reverie was shattered by another lurch at 64 DME. Over the intercom I heard the captain speak, "The right engine has quit. Call Anchorage; tell them we are turning back. Request a lower altitude."

I hesitated; the attitude gyro indicated we were in a 30-degree bank that was growing even steeper. The directional gyro was turning too fast. My thoughts were, "What's going on? Level the wings, damn it." I nudged the controls to slow our rate of roll.

"Anchorage Center, Skyvan . . . we've lost an engine. We're returning to Anchorage. Request a lower altitude," I called.

Center responded, "Skyvan . . . say again."

"Why aren't we following procedures for securing the engine?" I thought as I replied to center. "Skyvan . . . we've had an engine failure, we are returning to Anchorage, we're unable to maintain altitude; please stand by."

I wasn't worried. We had altitude and time, but I couldn't find a checklist. I told myself to start someplace. I asked the captain, "Do you want to feather the engine?"

"Yes, yes, feather the engine!" he replied. I was embarrassed to respond, "I don't know how. I haven't been trained." The captain reached up and feathered the right engine.

Seconds later the left engine quit. The captain feathered it. We glided silently through the clouds. I thought, "What a lousy place to die. Not here, not now."

"What do we do now?" I asked.

"Let's try a restart, unfeather the right engine," the captain said.

"How?"

"Push up!" he shouted.

He shoved the overhead T-handle. Nothing happened. I pushed up in imitation. I pushed again. I shoved my fist against each handle. They wouldn't budge. I reasoned both must have been frozen. The loadmaster handed me the aluminum logbook to use as a hammer but to no avail. The handles wouldn't budge.

I thanked God that at least the wings were still level. The captain tried again; he couldn't move either handle. I was furious that those thin rods wouldn't move.

Now we were at 9,500 feet, 3,500 feet below the minimum en route altitude. I looked at the captain. He was scanning for a hole in the clouds. It was hopeless; it was overcast to sea level and we were over mountains. I focused all my attention on the handles. I resisted the temptation to twist and break one. My thoughts were simple, "If I am going to die, then I'm going to go fighting, not sitting on my hands."

I asked the loadmaster to find a crowbar as I continued to pound with my clenched fist. The youngster handed me a steel bar. I wondered where he found it. He was the cool one. I was ready to pry the panel apart.

My mind raced with images of a crash landing in the glaciers below. I looked up to figure out where to place the bar. Suddenly the T-handle slot seemed magnified. For the first time I saw how the mechanism operated. I cursed myself, pulled it down and back and released the handle upward. The right engine unfeathered. I repeated the procedure to unfeather the left engine. Miraculously, the captain restarted both.

We began climbing again at 8,000 feet. We had descended 4,000 feet. Center called and said that our position was safe. I did not believe them; without a chart, I wasn't sure. But I figured we were still too near those mountains. I wanted altitude. I wanted to jettison the cargo. The captain said no. I was angry. *He* had turned the inlet melters on to melt the ice that had shut down the engines. *He* had been unable to feather the engines. Twenty minutes later, we were safely on the ground at Anchorage. I wanted to go home and have a beer.

Postscript: as a professional pilot, I offer no excuses for our actions during the flight. No checklist, no chart, unfamiliar with procedures in our own aircraft . . . we committed every possible mistake, but we were lucky and survived our incompetence.

Maybe that's what is meant by "light as a feather." Over mountainous Alaskan terrain in particular, the cockpit has to be shipshape for deft handling of an emergency. There's only so much a copilot can do.

In the next confession, by a military pilot, there's only so much abuse an old Lockheed T-33 can take.

It was a cool, cloudy Sunday at Malmstrom Air Force Base in Great Falls, Montana, when I was awakened by a telephone call from my squadron commander. Northwest Airlines was on strike and a senior noncommissioned officer needed to get to Pittsburgh, Pennsylvania—his mother was dying.

I said I'd be glad to take him in the backseat of a T-33, the trainer version of the old F-80 Shooting Star, used by NORAD as a target for intercept practice and as a general support aircraft. The T-Bird is an old veteran from the late 1940s—the ones we flew were 1956 and 1957 models—but it is fully aerobatic and cruises at a respectable 380 knots. Although it has a service ceiling of 47,000 feet, anything above Flight Level 400 is an effort.

I met the sergeant at the squadron building to put together some flying gear for him. We always kept some extra helmets and masks, and I loaned him a flight suit and jacket from my locker. I spent several minutes explaining how the oxygen system and intercom worked, and how we would handle certain emergencies. He was supposed to have a briefing by a life-support-system specialist, but there was no time for that. We went down to operations to get the weather and file a flight plan.

Using 600-mile legs, I planned to stop for refueling at Grand

Forks Air Force Base in North Dakota and Grissom Air Force Base in Peru, Indiana, before landing at Pittsburgh at about nine o'clock that night. A huge cold front with severe thunderstorms, however, was forecast to be centered over Grand Forks at the time of our arrival. The frontal line would be about 60 miles west of the base and the squall line preceding the front would be almost on top of it. It looked like a bumpy ride.

Having a passenger for the trip wouldn't help. Cruising at 35,000 to 39,000 feet, the T-Bird could pick its way around most of the bad weather even though it lacked radar. The sergeant had not had pressure-chamber training, however, so he was limited to a maximum cabin altitude of 10,500 feet, or 18,000 feet in the sort-of-pressurized T-33. We filed for 17,000 and went out to the airplane. There I reviewed all the normal and emergency procedures and helped him strap in and hook up the oxygen and radio leads. We had a smooth takeoff and a pleasant flight for the first hour. There isn't much real scenery between Great Falls and Grand Forks, but we were both enjoying the view.

As we approached Grand Forks, the fun came to an end. We were soon being bounced around in moderate to severe turbulence and were completely embedded in thick cumulus clouds. Rain showers streamed back over the cockpit. On the radio, several other airplanes were asking for radar vectors around the cells, especially the pilot of a light twin near our position at 8,000 feet who sounded as if he was in real trouble. We found out later that this aircraft had crashed in the storm, killing the occupants. I asked for an instrument approach to Grand Forks, but upon arrival we found we were ahead of the squall line. Although it was cloudy, visibility was good and the runway was dry. I concentrated on making a really good landing, since nonflying passengers always seem to judge the whole flight on that basis. While the line crew refueled the airplane, the sergeant and I retired to base operations for new weather, new flight planning and a Coke.

The weather officer on duty had nothing good to say. The

weather system was intensifying, and several severe thunderstorms and possible tornadoes were visible on the radar scan. The tops of the worst buildups were above 50,000 feet, but the level of general cloudiness topped at about 25,000. If we could get above it, he said, we should be able to pick our way around the worst of it. Unfortunately, the front was passing the base by then, and our climb-out would be through the middle of it. After 75 miles, though, we'd have clear sailing.

I went down to approach control to discuss the departure with them, and got the great news that the center was combined with the Air Defense SAGE radar system at Grand Forks, which does not paint any weather. I explained our problem to the sergeant and told him that for his own safety we'd have to wait a day, or bend the rules a little and go the first 100 miles at 30,000 feet. He had no problem with this, since he'd done well with the oxygen mask on the way over, and we reviewed the use of the equipment. I told him to keep talking with me often, and that way I would descend at once if I lost intercommunication with him.

When we went out to the airplane it was raining and the sky was intensely black. Thunder could be heard all around, and lightning was visible to the east. I cranked up and got us airborne.

It was immediately clear that we were in for a rough trip. Before we got to 3,000 feet we were in thick cloud and rain was ripping across us in sheets. The turbulence alternated between bumpy and severe, and as we went through 7,000 feet we began to pick up ice; eventually we were carrying about an inch. There was lightning everywhere. I reflected that this was the worst weather I'd ever been in. I wondered what the sarge was thinking, but was too busy with the departure to discuss it.

As we approached 24,000 feet, the heavy clouds fell away and we were in a land of giant white mushrooms. Towering cumulus buildups were visible in every direction, but we were above the thick, boiling stew of weather that had just seemed so oppressive.

"Well, Sarge," I said, "we should have clear sailing now!"

"Yessir," he replied.

Just then a most remarkable thing happened—the engine flamed out. There were no warning lights, bells or whistles. In fact, it got deathly quiet. My one comment was, "Sarge, we've just lost the engine." His only response was, "Yessir." You'd have thought we were talking about the price of beans. Then quickly and surely, I began the routine: *Gang start switch on, throttle-idle. Trim for 180 knots indicated airspeed for maximum glide*. The gang start system in the T-33 is the pilot's security blanket for flameouts. It turns on all the fuel pumps and gives starting fuel and ignition. I watched the gauges for indications of a start and I also kept an eye on the storm, into which we were rapidly descending again. When the engine lit a few seconds later, it *really* lit. There was a loud thump, the rpm started back up, and the exhaust gas temperature rose rapidly, finally pegging at 900°—the normal maximum starting temperature is 710°. Engineers later told me the tailpipe temperature must have been more than 1,200°, as evidenced by crystallization of some of the stainless steel parts. The shroud immediately collapsed upon the turbine blades, producing a continuous grating sound. The overheat warning light came on for a bit, then went out. I correctly surmised that I'd better not plan on anything more than idle power for the rest of the flight. By that time we were back in the clouds, flying by seat-of-the-pants and needle-ball-airspeed. The normal IFR instruments driven by the AC power supply had not come back on line.

I asked center for an immediate vector to the nearest runway and a Rapcon frequency. I got a rough vector, then called Fargo Approach at the Air National Guard Base 10 or 15 miles away. They gave me the good news—no radar. By this time I was finding it difficult to fly the bird in the storm with no power and with limited instruments, so I began looking for a hole. We went down a shaft that was lighter than the rest. I leveled off under the cloud bank at 2,000 feet. I told my friend at Rapcon that I could see some white oil tanks, and asked for advice.

"Those are probably the ones south of town," he said, so I turned due north on the standby magnetic compass and watched the airspeed rapidly bleeding away.

"I see the town!" I cried. "Where's the runway?"

"Three miles north." Would we make it? I started to review the ejection procedure with the sergeant, but he said, "I'd rather not eject, sir." I was with him all the way. I saw the runway and was just able to make one turn to final and lower flaps over the overrun. We did a full-stall landing 1,000 feet down and turned off about two-thirds of the way down the runway. We heard clanking noises during the roll-out, which turned out to be assorted engine parts falling out of the tailpipe and out of a 2-1/2-foot hole that had been blown through the side of the fuselage about halfway down the tail section. A large red fire/rescue truck appeared just as we turned off the active.

The disposition of the accident took several weeks. A filter in the automatic fuel control had iced up, causing the initial failure. The explosive restart was the result of a sloppy recent overhaul of the airplane. The gang start system had been improperly realigned, allowing raw fuel to pile up and eventually flash. The T-Bird was considered unsalvageable, and has since been used for fire department training at Fargo. In the end, it was decided that I deserved an air medal for the flying job in saving the airplane and my passenger, and a court martial for violating flight regulations by taking a passenger without pressure-chamber training above 18,000 feet. My commander, a very reasonable man, suggested we just forget the whole thing instead. So I did.

Are You Kidding!

Flying is a heady mixture of pleasing predictability, occasionally surprising unpredictability, sheer awe and sometimes just plain, well, strangeness. There can be a funny side to it, too, although the pilot may not realize it at the time. But he might be magnanimous enough to share the experience later, as have the pilots in this collection of strange happenings.

We start with a confused soul who is left wondering how the likelihood of a gear-up landing depends on the amount of coffee he drank at breakfast. Yup, we did say strange.

The law of probability is malevolent. It is causality with a perverse sense of humor. Stated simply, it holds that anything that can possibly go wrong will. It is usually attributed to a gremlin named Murphy. More often than not, Murphy's principle is the faintest essence, a speck of black ink that thins and spreads throughout the fabric of events, touching every strand, altering both color and texture, yet invisible except in the strongest light—or in retrospect.

These thoughts had come to mind during my walk-around inspection of a Cessna 210. Cessna makes nice airplanes. They are easy to fly and have few bad habits. But this particular early model, I knew, had a reputation for landing-gear problems. So it was that, as I peered into the wheel wells at the hydraulic plumbing, electrical solenoids and mechanical latches (strange how delicate and frail they suddenly looked), I thought of Murphy's Law.

I was reminded of Murphy again after takeoff, as the landing gear thumped into the wells. Of course, the retraction *would* be perfectly normal. Murphy is far too subtle to introduce abnormalities this early in the program. No, the best would come last, and I began to count the minutes before I would need to extend the gear. After all, it wouldn't do to lunge for the gear switch before it was time to use it and show Murphy that he had me unnerved. Besides, I certainly couldn't let my companion on this morning's flight see that I had doubts about something as basic as whether or not the landing gear would extend.

My mental state was such that when I finally moved the little wheel-shaped switch down and the gear did nothing in response, I felt not the slightest flicker of surprise. The hyrdaulic pump made purposeful noises, but there was none of the thumping and bumping that normally indicate extending landing gear, and the gear-up light never wavered.

I looked over at my companion, noting the surprise and concern in his expression. It was obvious that he had not been thinking about Murphy; it would be my unpleasant duty to broaden his horizons. I again placed the gear switch in the down position, and once more we listened to the pump motor's plaintive whine. My passenger's expression then clouded with suspicion, as though I were perpetrating a cruel practical joke. Rather than answer him directly, I called the tower and told them that we would be leaving the pattern for a while.

That convinced him of my sincerity: at these prices, ours would be very expensive amusement.

As we swung away from the field and gained altitude, he opened the airplane's handbook and began reading out loud. We both knew the primary emergency procedure, of course; what I was hoping to find was a contingency plan that would match the conditions we were seeing. The handbook assumes that the electric motor has failed and explains how to extend the gear manually using the hand pump. But our electric pump seemed to be working beautifully, a supposition that was confirmed a moment later when we carefully went through the emergency gear-extension sequence with the hand pump and accomplished exactly nothing.

Round one to Murphy.

It was at this point that I began to appreciate just how little I knew about the landing-gear system. Could it be that we were futilely pumping the gear against the uplocks? Or perhaps we had a leak and were pumping the fluid overboard before enough pressure could be generated to start the sequence. There is no pressure gauge, but there is a reservoir under the instrument panel. While my companion plunged under the panel to look at the fluid level, I decided to get some advice.

Working through the local unicom, I was soon talking to a mechanic. His voice reflected even amounts of curiosity and dread, and I recalled that just yesterday he had completed a 100-hour inspection on this airplane, so his signature was probably all over the logbooks.

It didn't take much time to explain what we'd done and even less to tell what we'd accomplished. He promised to get back to us with some answers. Meanwhile, preceded by a lot of grunting and swearing, my companion had emerged from under the panel with a small dipstick attached to a pressure stopper.

"According to this," he said, "the reservoir's almost empty." Sure enough, only the very bottom of the stick had fluid on it. I relayed this bit of information to the people on the ground, then sat back to wait.

Fortunately, we had started this little adventure with full tanks, so there wasn't any particular hurry—at these reduced power settings, we could stay up for a long time. Actually, the idea of landing the airplane gear-up hadn't really sunk in yet. Murphy's Law notwithstanding, I was sure the mechanics would come up with the magic formula. I am a devout clean liver who is always kind to dogs, old people and small children and, therefore, did not deserve such a rotten fate.

By now we were beginning to attract some attention. A Beech Baron came on the frequency with an offer to help. He quickly joined up with us and reported that the gear doors were tightly closed; there was no sign of hydraulic fluid on the underside.

Then the mechanic came back on the frequency.

"Everyone that I've talked to seems to think you're too low on fluid. Is there anything in the airplane you can use to fill the reservoir?"

A quick search revealed a few cans of dog food and an almost empty bottle of windshield cleaner: we were definitely fluid poor.

Or were we? The radio came alive once again.

"You know, it doesn't have to be hydraulic fluid. Any fluid would work. . . ."

"Do you mean that whether or not we get the gear down is going to depend on how much coffee we drank this morning?"

The radio emitted a high, wailing tone as several transmitters were keyed at once; then the noise stopped abruptly, leaving one voice, "And don't worry about damaging the system; it can always be flushed out later." The voice was so serious that it was obvious its owner hadn't recognized the double entendre.

As I moved back to a spot between the first and second rows of seats, trying to find a comfortable position for an act that was at once very familiar and extremely foreign, I looked at the plastic bottle in my hand and thought: this is truly Murphy's finest hour. I shook my head, and, with my companion looking demurely the other way, filled the small plastic bottle, feeling as foolish as I have ever felt in my entire life.

The chase plane swung in close to watch the underside. We both stared at the tiny gear switch with a hypnotic fascination as I moved it into the down position. The pump emitted a steady whine, the yellow light returned our stare unblinkingly, and the Baron reported what we had already guessed: nothing.

Round two to Murphy.

The mechanic came on with a new suggestion: "Try some abrupt maneuvering—maybe you can shake it loose."

"Why not?" I shrugged and, after the chase plane moved away, began pulling the airplane into progressively steeper turns, increasing the centrifugal force until I felt the first nibblings of a stall. The landing gear remained unperturbed. My companion suggested going from positive to negative Gs as rapidly as possible while he worked the hand pump. Being careful to stay well below maneuvering speed because of our light weight, I pulled the nose up to near vertical and pushed it over until we were shoved up against the seat belts and the engine stumbled from uneven fuel flow.

My companion muttered an oath and stopped pumping long enough to pull his seat belt tighter. We kept going up and down, alternately pressed into the seat and floating away from it; had we left a smoke trail, it would have taken the form of a textbook sine wave. Finally, it became obvious that we were not accomplishing anything. The chase plane quickly confirmed this; everything was still buttoned up tight.

Round three to Murphy.

Frustration began to tie an angry knot inside me, as I considered the years of development that went into this aircraft; the number of presumably talented people whose job it was to design a simple, trouble-free landing gear; and the time that this system has been in service and presumably debugged. At that point in my reflections, I grabbed the pump handle and began savagely banging it up and down, venting my growing anger on the inanimate object closest at hand.

Several things happened at once: the pressure resisting the handle's movement changed abruptly, my companion reported that fluid was fountaining out of the reservoir, and the chase plane shouted that the main gear doors were beginning to open. This was welcome but unnecessary information, for the pump handle's changing pressure told me that the system was finally working. After about ten strokes, it occurred to me to try the electric pump. After I had reset the circuit breaker, the pump smoothly took up the load and extended the gear. We were once again flying a complete airplane.

As we headed back to the airport, the mood in the cockpit was jubilant; the sudden releasing of tension left us with a heady sense of victory.

I should have known better.

I mean, just because we had the airplane back on the ground didn't mean that Murphy had packed up and left. Nor had our successful gear extension made us victors. When the battle's outcome has been determined solely by fate (or Murphy), there are no winners or losers; there are only participants.

I never did get a definite explanation of what had gone wrong with the gear mechanism; worse, we never found out exactly why the gear finally did extend—which, of course, was Murphy's knockout punch.

Today the airplane sits on our flight line, taunting me to fly it again, and I can't shake the thought that Murphy is biding his time, waiting for the right moment to bring this chain of events to its conclusion: sooner or later I am going to belly-land that airplane.

There's an even more disturbing possibility. Am I unable to treat this as an insignificant mechanical incident because I had been brooding about Murphy's Law before the trouble began? Is it possible such brooding activates the law?

If that's true—if the key to Pandora's box is nothing more than the touch of a thought upon your mind—then I've done you, gentle reader, a great disservice: you should never have read this article.

Murphy was on vacation while this pilot propped his Bellanca Scout. Murphy wasn't needed; this guy was doing just fine lousing up the process on his own.

I am not the first pilot to be run down by his own aircraft; but I may be one of the most experienced—a dubious honor. It was 3:00 P.M. when I arrived at my dirt strip on a perfectly gorgeous October day in Colorado. At Memorial Airport, my intended destination twelve miles north, two of my students were waiting for a lesson at 4:00 P.M. It would be a ten-minute flight at the most. I did a thorough preflight that included removing the tie-down ropes.

Near the end of my spray season some three weeks earlier, I

had had alternator problems. Since I'd had no other spray airplane available then and did not wish to interrupt service to my customers, I had simply shut down the electrical system and continued to work by propping the aircraft. Now the alternator was out for repairs and hand-propping was still the order of the day.

Why I had untied the aircraft during my preflight, I don't know. Habit? Haste? That was my first mistake. I have propped aircraft with a safety pilot at the controls countless times, and I have even made it a part of training new pilots. I recall all too well having once been stranded for several hours at St. Louis's Lambert Field because I couldn't find anyone who could or would prop the Cessna 172 I was flying. Since that time I have propped aircraft alone safely hundreds of times in the thirty-eight years I've been flying. Don't misunderstand me; I am not advocating or condoning propping an airplane without a safety pilot. It has simply been a professional necessity.

Two or three turns of the prop usually started the Scout, but this time it had been sitting. I placed a U-shaped chock around the front right tire. Magneto switches off, mixture rich, throttle fully retarded, then about six to eight turns of the prop. Walking around the spray booms to the cabin, I threw both mags on, cracked the throttle and propped it several times. Nothing. This procedure of alternately priming it a little more each time, then pulling it through—mags off, of course—to clear out excess fuel in the cylinders, continued for some twenty-five minutes without so much as a sputter.

Although I was running short of time, I had enough of it to get in my truck and drive back. But I had to get in that last try: mags off, throttle full forward, mixture lean to correct possible overpriming, then pull it through four times. I walked back to the cabin, switched the mags on, pushed the mixture full rich and retarded the throttle to the fully closed position. Or did I?

On the second turn of the prop, the engine caught, but with an alarming roar. By the time I had leaped out of the way and scrambled to the right wingtip and started toward the cabin, the Scout had jumped the chock and was accelerating rapidly across my newly planted wheat field. I grabbed the door frame and ran desperately, trying to get one foot on the step. It was hopeless. I was being dragged wildly by the aircraft as it began a pronounced turn to the left, and to hang on any longer was to invite disaster. When I relaxed my grip, I could feel flesh tearing on metal as my hand caught on a jagged edge. When I fell away, I hit the hard, dry clods face first. I jumped to my feet spitting dirt and blood.

The Scout was roaring back toward me, and I either had to get out of its way or be chewed up. My brain was sifting every possible way to get back to the cabin, where I could shut down the engine. Without endangering my life, it would be impossible—like trying to run down a loose buzz saw. I could only stand there, helpless, and wait for it to flip over on its back. After crossing the runway and striking an embankment, it flipped and I breathed a sigh of relief.

Slowly, not believing that I could have made such mistakes, I approached the silent, inverted hulk of my hardworking little Scout. I checked for fuel leakage and turned off the switches. A twisted propeller, smashed windshield and broken rudder were the only outward signs of damage, but there had to be more. It turned out to be more than $5,000 worth.

How fortunate that I learned this lesson on a remote landing strip with plenty of open space.

Why hadn't I left the tailwheel rope tied? Obviously, I had not retarded the throttle, and indeed I later found it to be halfway open. But perhaps my most serious mistake had been in not taking care of a defective part before trying to operate the aircraft.

I had always thought of myself as a thorough, cautious, experienced pilot. Now I have been rightfully humbled.

Perhaps the pilot wished for a while that his airplane had done a thorough job of it and actually run him over. At least he wouldn't have been around to own up to what had happened.

The next pilot felt pretty foolish, too, as he sat on the airport in the cockpit of his Mooney waving a flashlight at passing cars.

It was Christmas Day and snowing at Altoona, Pennsylvania. I had flown there on December 23 to spend the holiday with friends. The snow fizzled out by lunchtime, and by midafternoon I was back at the airport, broom in hand, removing three inches of snow and ice from the Mooney. There was a brisk 15-knot wind, and the temperature was hovering around 23° F. Still, no matter—I'd soon be on my way back home to Lakewood, New Jersey. Flight service advised that the route—via Harrisburg, Philadelphia and the shoreline—was VFR and forecast to remain 3,000 to 4,000 scattered, variable to broken; visibility was 10 miles and surface temperature 45° F.

Having removed the bulk of the winter weather, I went to open the cabin door. The lock was frozen solid. An airport on Christmas Day is as deserted as an ice cap—everything at the airport was closed, and I had nothing with which to deice or heat the stubborn lock. But the baggage hatch was accessible, so I loaded my gear and prepared to leave. Once I'd explained to my friends how to secure the hatch, I crawled through it and weaved my way into the front seat. With everything checked out, I took off for Lakewood at about 4:00 P.M.

Apart from moderate turbulence, the flight to Lakewood was good VFR. I checked in with Harrisburg Approach while passing through and contacted Philadelphia Approach west of Bucktown Intersection. Leaving the Philadelphia sector, I monitored McGuire into Lakewood, but I didn't establish contact. The wind was gusting to 35 knots directly across the runway as I lined up for a night approach on Runway 24 at Lakewood. I was almost down when a gust lifted the ship about 20 feet. I went around again. This time the Mooney settled as if on eggs, and I taxied to the terminal apron.

Lakewood at 6:00 P.M. on Christmas night, with a blistering wind howling across the flats, was totally deserted. Now, for those who are unfamiliar with Mooneys, there's no way to unlock the cabin door or open the baggage hatch from inside. I was a prisoner, encased in an aluminum cell.

I taxied to a point where I could see the highway that passes the airport, so that I might catch the eye of a driver. For two hours I waved a flashlight at the cars, but to no avail. No one was about to investigate some nut waving a flashlight from a parked airplane.

Blind transmissions on 122.8 were equally ineffective so, much as I disliked the idea of challenging the crosswinds again, I decided to hop across to Miller Airport at Toms River, where there is usually a police guard. I arrived there at about 8:00 P.M. and found the place as deserted as Lakewood, but with more lights.

I knew I could fly back to North Philadelphia and get someone to unlock the door, but decided on a shorter route. Having taken off from Miller, I turned on the transponder and called McGuire Approach. I described my predicament and asked for the police to be sent to Lakewood, so that they could set me free. In a few minutes approach called back, confirming that the law would be there promptly, and vectored me to Lakewood. He showed concern, wished me luck and asked that I phone him when the fiasco was resolved.

By now I was grooved in on the crosswind landings, and the last one was a piece of cake. I taxied to the terminal ramp and within minutes the officers arrived. I passed the door key through the storm window, and that was that. Freedom! I taxied to the hangar, and the police obligingly stood by until I had put the aircraft away and was ready to leave.

I called both the McGuire controller and the Lakewood police to thank them when I got home. It's hard to beat good communications.

And a merry Christmas to you, too, Officer. The next pilot's brush with the law was not quite so amicable: he ended up in court for practicing crosswind landings . . . sort of.

I looked at the wrecked Luscombe and wanted to be sick. The prop was bent, the wingtips drooped, the empennage was twisted and there was a wrinkle the size of two hands aft of the cabin where the fuselage bent. The left main gear leg, the one that had struck the mound in the barley field, was bent back parallel to the cabin. I was unscratched.

I had been practicing crosswind landings. Everything about the wheels-on approach and touchdown had gone well, up to the time the tailwheel began to settle. As I came back on the stick, the ship began to weathercock, setting up a potential ground loop, and the airplane accelerated almost to flying speed. I was off the paved runway, running parallel to it in the field the airport leases to the barley farmer, but in another second, I would be airborne and the Luscombe would be back in its element. Then the left main hit that hidden mound of earth.

Luscombe N2560K is an A-model that has been modified to an E. At that time, it was a rented ship, the personal property of the FBO and his partner. The only thing the fixed-base operator loved better than that airplane was his dog. After the accident, he never had any doubt that he would rebuild the ship. It took him almost two years, but rebuild it he did.

Naturally, he was insured. There was the matter of the $500 deductible, but I paid that. It took a while, but I finally squared with him.

The insurance was something else. The average value of Luscombes, according to *Trade-a-Plane,* was well over $2,200. The maximum policy the insurance company would write was $1,800, and after subtracting $500 because it had been an "in-motion" accident, the policy would pay off only $1,300 maximum. The insurance company was willing to pay this, but that meant they got the wreck. My friend bid at the auction for his own plane and paid $500 for it.

The insurance adjustor who came around to interview me was very nice. He was much more interested in the incident than the GADO had been. Several months later, I found out the reason when the marshal came and gave me a subpoena.

My lawyer explained the nature of the suit to me. The insurance company had suffered a loss that it would try to show was caused by my negligence. According to my lawyer, I would have to prove in court that I had not acted in an unreasonable and imprudent manner. I declined a jury trial because I couldn't have afforded the costs of one if I'd lost, and I thought I had a strong case that would appeal to a judge's legal eye. At the last minute I had a lucky break. The case was assigned to a judge who had flown during the war. During the trial, I found out that he had been an aviation cadet and that he had won his wings in a Stearman, so he knew all about ground loops and taildraggers.

The lawyer for the insurance company called one witness, a private pilot with "about 100 hours" in T-6s. He swore under oath that it was better to try to three-point a taildragger in a gusting crosswind than to try to wheel it on. He admitted under cross-examination that he had never flown a Luscombe, a point my lawyer seemed to think was important. I hope he never tries a Swift, either, if he likes to three-point in gusting crosswinds.

I, too, called a single witness—the FBO who owned the airplane. He wasn't permitted to testify that he had okayed my taking the Luscombe that day; I was pilot in command and I couldn't put my responsibilities off onto anybody else. Also, I could not bring into evidence the FAA's decision not to cite me or even order a flight-proficiency check.

Then I testified. My lawyer felt there could be no harm in it. The insurance company's lawyer had already introduced my statement to the investigator as evidence, and it would work to my advantage to present myself as a reasonable person and a knowledgeable pilot on the stand. That statement I had made to the insurance investigator was a crucial point. Without it, there probably wouldn't have been enough evidence to bring suit.

After the testimony was in, the insurance company's lawyer got to make a statement. Then my lawyer got to make one. But the insurance company lawyer got the last licks: he said it was unreasonable and imprudent for me to have gone up on a day when there was a crosswind in order to practice crosswind landings. He said that crosswind landings were something a pilot reads about and attempts only when he has to, not something he risks a valuable airplane to practice.

While I was reeling from the thrust of this final summation, the judge announced that he was taking the matter under consideration and swept from the room, almost before the bailiff could give the order "all rise." A week later, my attorney's secretary called to say that she had a note from the clerk of the court, announcing that the insurance company had lost. My legal expenses equalled the cost of a half year of flying.

What did I learn? I learned that hull insurance has its limitations, and that once the propeller starts turning you are expected to understand the fine-print parts. If you owe money on your ship, you have to have hull insurance, of course, but the combined effects of a deductible amount once you're in motion—when most accidents happen—and the insurance companies' habit of declaring a total wreck and taking title to the airplane would seem to make it worthwhile only if you leave your airplane parked.

I also learned that any insurance company can press subrogation suits, calling "expert" witnesses and crying negligence.

How, I wonder, would a less knowledgeable judge have reacted to the charge that practicing crosswind landings is negligence?

Case dismissed. But the lesson is valuable in illustrating some of the tricks the insurance trade will pull when it's time for them to pay up. The pilot got stung. So did the next one—by one of a horde of wasps that had hitched a ride.

Sometimes I dream a strange dream, where I'm awakened by the shattering silence of my airplane's engine quitting—that's all, just silence. Actually, the dream isn't so strange, for in my work for an airplane repair shop, I fly many airplanes with freshly rebuilt engines. I break them in properly and troubleshoot the problems that occasionally show up the first few hours after overhaul. Ninety percent of them are petty annoyances, such as oil leaks and minor vibrations, which the owner would prefer not to worry about.

One day, Doug, the owner of the repair shop; Tom, a friend of his; and I delivered an overhauled and freshly painted Cherokee 150 to its proud owner. For the return trip, we climbed into a borrowed Cessna 182 that Doug was taking in for some minor repairs and a check ride. We had to prop the airplane, as it had sat unused for some months on a crop duster strip.

After a quick takeoff and climb-out, we were above the haze at 3,000 feet. It was sunny on top, and the cabin began to heat, so I reached overhead and opened the air vent. As I was enjoying a face full of cool fresh air, I saw Doug reach for his vent. Instead of a rush of cool air, a large wad of squirming, angry wasps—undoubtedly the nastiest winged creatures I've ever seen—emerged from the vent. They had obviously been comfortably nested in the vent, undisturbed for a long time, and made dormant by the cool outside air temperature.

Soon, our uninvited guests began to warm themselves in the cabin. They became a bit restless (they weren't the only ones), and we became convenient landing strips for their short flights. We had already begun a hasty descent, while trying to keep the wasps away from our faces and maintain our composure. Doug was flying when he suddenly got stung. I hadn't been stung yet, so I took over the controls as Doug tried to rid himself of the wasps. Tom, who was sitting in the back, was attempting to keep them out of our hair and from going down the backs of our collars. Unlike bees, wasps will sting repeatedly.

At 600 feet, Doug finally killed his attacker and again assumed the flying chores. The wasps were now seemingly content to sun themselves on the inside of the windshield, with a few doing chandelles and lazy eights about our heads. I watched one dance on my arm, hoping he was just doing his run-up before takeoff, and praying that it wasn't a prelude to deep arterial research. I sighed in relief as he took to the air. However, after the first go-around, he set up a neat left-hand pattern and turned final for Doug's ear.

I've learned from farm life that you never swat a wasp. It can attack you much faster than you can run, while at the same time telegraphing your position to the rest of the swarm, which will soon follow suit. So there we sat, trying to be as calm as possible.

Doug knew of a crop duster strip in the area and headed toward it, while I busied myself giving some of our fellow aviators the brush-off. Suddenly, the strip was dead ahead; we were so low we had to climb to flare. Finally, the wheels touched down, and before the prop stopped, the three of us were out of the door.

As we shakily stood outside, looking into the wasp-filled cockpit, we all made a vow. *Always* check the air vents before a flight, especially if the airplane has sat unused for a long time. A wasp sting near the eyes can blind a person in seconds. At the least, uninvited guests doing touch-and-goes on your nose can be very distracting, even with two pilots at the controls.

Learning to Love It

When it's all going right, flying is hard to beat for producing a sense of sheer satisfaction. Half the pleasure comes from recalling the pain of building your skills to the point at which they are this satisfying. Sometimes in training, it seemed that however hard you tried, the task was beyond you. Such is the satisfaction of safely completing, for instance, the first instrument approach to minimums, a feat that avenges the frustration of all those wavering needles during your training. It is an exquisite feeling to have defied the apparent impossibility of traveling from A to B without ever seeing anything in between.

While the more terrifying moments of flight can show us our existence in a different light, so can the more stirring moments kindle an inner warmth that somehow nothing else can spark. Some pilots have the gift of sharing that warmth, and their stories follow, some in the humorous vein of grateful hindsight, some more personal.

I need to share this one with you while the hair, hide and hooves are still on it. While the sweat of it is not yet washed off and precludes, through our covenant, the reckless lying of survivors, the bravado of tomorrow. I have just made my first really low approach: "300 feet, one-quarter mile and fog, sky obscured, runway visual range 4,000 feet. . . . Did you copy the weather, Niner-Six-Zero?" Do you want to drink of this cup? Are you awake? Are you sure this is what you want to enter into? Oh, gentle tower man. Later, after you had held me like a mother holds a tiny babe in arms and crooned to me, and I was rolling and alive on cement, you did tell me that at the moment of my touchdown, the sky had lowered still more and what we really had was 200 feet, and the lowest decision height that I can find on the plate for Beaumont-Port Arthur, Jefferson County, Texas, is 216 feet (200). Oh, Lordy.

Understand, I did not overtly bargain for this. My personal

decision height is 800 feet and 1 mile, because I am green and an amateur at this, and until this day there were many important things yet unresolved in my mind. But overriding it all was the simple fact that low approaches really scare hell out of me. And, until I contacted Beaumont Approach at Honey Intersection, still on top in the drying brightness of the sun, I was expecting 800 and 4. I got it in writing from the FSS at my departure point, just two hours ago at Love, Dallas.

There was that business of Houston ATC, who was one of those garglers who sat too close to the mike and ripped off all his lingo as if we were all Delta captains with Collins flight directors to pave the way and one good man with nothing more to do than listen close on a high-powered radio and try to make English out of what he was spouting. This Houston ATC got peeved with me because the Cessna was slow and rented and I was not high-keyed to the fact that Niner-Six-Zero was me. How could he know that what I was doing was putting on my buckler and my shield and preparing to do battle when my moment of truth came in that white ice cream below? My mind was often far away. And once, when he got churlish with me, I got churlish with him; in my most easy Texican, I asked, "Hew-ston, cain't you talk like thi-yus?" It was chancy, but it cooled his machine gun some. When he handed me off to Beaumont Approach, we were both thinking good riddance.

And when Beaumont let me down into the stuff, I decided this was not the time for false pride and to take this man to my warm side and tell him how it really is. "Beaumont, take me slow. This will be the lowest approach I ever made." And that's when I felt the humanness of the man in the cement tower peering into his green scope at the man in the fragile aluminum who was about to bet his old arse and all of its fixtures. He took me slow. Let me tell you now and tell all the high honchos of the FAA who this man is. He is Glen Martinka. I never met him, never pressed the flesh, but for a while that night, we were brothers.

Glen took me down to 2,500 and then down to 1,500, and in my mind's eye I could see all the refineries and their tall stacks superimposed on the opaque grayness ahead. Glen kept calling out targets to me—yes, there was other traffic. An Air Force Herky Bird was over here sharpening the blade of skill against the stone of danger. And unbelievably, there was some klutz out in a Grumman Traveler shooting approaches. Jerry's Aviation. Whoever it was, they must have cods to carry in a wheelbarrow to play on a day like this. "Beaumont, thanks for the traffic reports, but I can't even see my own wingtips." And Metro went barreling out for Houston, ho hum, just another day. Pros, those guys, peapatch pros, the great captains of tomorrow; but man, for me, I was at the cinema, watching in disbelief my own flesh and blood about to descend to 200 feet in fog. Part of my mind leaned back, munching popcorn, enjoying the show. Part of it was trying to hem up the localizer, and sweat was running free, between 110 and 140 degrees.

And Glen came in with, "You are at the localizer and cleared to land," and I realized that he had done all he could for me, and the moment of truth was at hand. Hear me, I'm no kamikaze; I had heard them tell the Herky Bird that Ellington was 700. I had a Plan Two: a missed approach and a night in some plastic motel in Houston. But I was committed, too. I must see the Bull. At last, now, after all these months of imagined terror, I must call him out. Toro! Toro!

Oh, why'n hell can't I hold a good localizer course? It's a learned skill, that's why, and I have gotten rusty to its subtle tones. Sinking into grayness, I made it academic. I was back at Bob Marsh Aviation in the simulator. It is all academic. If I don't make it, I can just flick off the switches and get out and face the sneers. Also, I was thinking, this will be sudden and not hurt much. Also thinking, in the next 20 seconds I am going to find out something I very much need to know. And so I descended, splitting my mind between the wandering needles of glideslope, localizer and all that. Reasoning, rationalizing with myself and betting nothing less than life, sweet life.

Do you know that the earth greens the obscurity when you are near her? A dark, dank greenness of earth. I knew. I was aware of her closeness; playing fortissimo with the rudders. Oh, gentle Cessna, mother of all aircraft, gentle, broad-winged bird, forgive us our trespasses. Earth was nigh. And then the lights. The crucifix of lights. Not all the candles burning yellow in St. Peter's could be more holy than this. "I got the lights." Hell, I could have landed on a postage stamp from there. What matter 4,000 feet range? What matter that I could not see across the field in the fog? Stearmans, Cubs, Airknockers, I can land short. And I was still holding Glen's hand. I had asked him not to make me change to the tower at the marker for that is the most crucial time, and no time to be playing with the radio. Glen Martinka carried me to the ramp, like a father holding up his newborn son.

I am curious. Even to death, always curious about life and all its processes. I took my pulse. One hundred and sixteen over a normal southern-boy 72. Not bad; they don't call in the astronauts until the pulse reaches 155. I was well below the screaming point. But the hands shook. The linemen laughed, "I don't think you are ready to repair any watches." Right.

To put your life in danger from time to time breeds a saneness in dealing with day-to-day trivialities. My personal minimums are still 800 and 1 mile, but the terror factor is gone.

That first instrument approach to minimums can easily be more heady than first solo. The acid knowledge that certain disaster lurked so close is what makes the surge of satisfaction so strong upon its safe completion. Some pilots, like Bax, can put it all in writing, too.

When the next story came into the office in 1980, we knew we had to use it somewhere. It made a very different, very moving

ILAFFT. Lee Dalton had placed a For Sale *ad for his old 172, and he was giving it a last clean before the new owner came in the morning.*

It had been one of those perfect days of late summer. Hot during the mid part of the day, the air had tempered with evening until the slight breeze was comfortably cool against my T-shirt. The shadows were stretching, and the grass and the trees were taking on that special golden quality that seems to go along with days of blue skies and puffy white clouds. I had come out to the airport after work and was wiping the drips of oil, smudges of dust and droppings of birds from the aluminum skin of the old Cessna 172. The new owner was coming in the morning, and I wanted the airplane to look its best.

I was crawling under the belly when I saw him standing beside his bicycle just inside the fence. He was rather small for a boy of ten or eleven or maybe even twelve. I had seen him standing by the fence several times before, standing and watching the comings and goings of the airplanes and their pilots. I didn't pay much attention to him, though, and kept working on the stubborn stain spreading aft from the exhaust stack. When I looked up again, I was a little surprised to find him standing only about ten feet away.

I rolled out from under the belly and nodded a greeting to him. He nodded back and edged a little closer. I started wiping down the left strut, watching out of the corner of my eye as he inched closer and closer until he was within reach of the propeller. But he kept his hands carefully beside him and looked toward the airplane, his eyes following the line of its fuselage and wing. His face was quiet and solemn under tousled brown hair. He didn't say anything, but in the dark corner of my memory, something woke up. "Would you like to look it over?" I asked, without really thinking.

His eyes snapped around toward me as though I had startled him. A small smile flashed across his mouth and then was replaced by the same serious line, but his eyes had a different light in them as he nodded his head just ever so slightly. He followed me around, eyes taking in every detail, carefully keeping his hands in pockets or folded behind his back. That old, old memory stirred and kicked a little, and I reassured him, "You can touch it. You won't hurt it."

He wasn't sure, but he put a timid hand forward and touched an elevator. It moved and he drew back, looking at me to see if he was in trouble. By way of answer, I raised and lowered the elevator and explained its purpose. The memory stirred again and I said, "But then, you probably already knew that, didn't you?"

He nodded and answered in a little voice, "Yes, I read all the books about airplanes." So I let him lead me around, and he pointed out and named all the parts, though he had trouble pronouncing aileron when we rounded the wingtip.

I opened the door. "Here, look inside." He approached the door as one would approach a most holy altar, and his eyes wore a look of perfect awe. He stood and stared and kept his hands perfectly corralled. I gave him a little nudge in the back and said, "Go ahead. Climb in."

Once more the memory stirred, and I thought for a moment that I could see another little boy climbing shyly into another airplane so many years ago. I remembered for a second just exactly how he felt. He settled himself in the seat, and I slid it forward saying, "You can touch it. There's nothing you can hurt as long as you don't flip any of the switches."

His eyes ran back and forth over the panel and the memory moved closer to the front of my head. "You fly for a while," I said, "and I'll go back to polishing." My rag flicked over the aluminum while I kept an eye on the cockpit. He grew bolder, and here and there a control surface move in response to pressure from a small hand. I was still polishing the top of the fuselage when my airplane took off without me, soaring past the ladder and over the treetops to some imaginary rendezvous with fate.

My rag slowed down and finally stopped as I listened to the engine noises coming from the cockpit and followed the course of the flight by watching the wing and tail surfaces as they rose and fell, tossing and pirouetting the airplane through loops and rolls and chandelles and split-S's as the pilot fought bravely to escape the Messerschmitts and Fokkers, or the MiGs and SAMs. I heard the machine guns chattering and the rockets whooshing away, and the memory rolled and looped and took me back to that other little boy twisting the wheel of his father's very earth-bound 1950 Ford as it flew among the clouds and fought the battles or turned into a thundering silver airliner. Suddenly, there was an odd tightness in my throat, and misty fog began to settle between my eyes and the trees across the fence by the road.

I blinked, and walked to the door and interrupted the battle. "Move over," I said gruffly, "and we'll go fly this thing."

He sat very still for a moment, then scrambled into the other seat. I climbed in, slid him forward, strapped him down, recited the checklist and started the engine.

We taxied out to the end of the grass for the run-up. Then we lined up and I asked, "Ready?" He nodded, but I noticed he was holding the seat with both hands, and white knuckles were showing as I pushed the throttle forward. We rolled and took off, and when we started the pattern turn I saw him stiffen for a second, then relax. Leaving the pattern, we climbed out over hills bathed in the glow of the evening light as his eyes drifted out the window by his side.

Suddenly, he bounced in his seat and started pointing out of the window and chattering at me. It took a second for me to understand what he was shouting. "My house! It's my house! I can see my house down there!" I racked the airplane into a tight right turn, and he saw his house and his friend's house and his school and the playground and the creek and the woods and everything else important in his world before we rolled level again and set off in search of a low cloud.

I spotted one and began climbing toward it. I had him kneel on the seat so he could see over the panel, and I put his hands on the wheel in front of him and showed him how the airplane would respond to his wishes while my feet worked the rudder for him. We reached the cloud and he flew around it and over it and under it, laughing in delight as the tendrils of white whipped past the Plexiglas. We swung back for another pass, and the memory of the other boy lying on his back by the creek bank while his mind played in the clouds grew stronger.

We played with the clouds until they started to show a golden pink and the ground was turning a gentle blue. A few lights began to flicker on to remind me it was time to go.

The wheels brushed the grass, the gear rumbled over the rough spots and we taxied to the hangar, where the propeller spun to a stop. The two pilots sat in silence for a moment or two. The smaller one stirred and said, "It's getting dark," and the bigger one said, "Yes, you'd better be heading for home." He nodded and climbed slowly out.

As he started to leave he stopped, turned and said quietly, but surely, "Thank you. I'm going to be a pilot, you know. Someday." Then he was on his way, and I watched him pedal down the dirt road I had pedaled so long ago on those summer afternoons, when I had stood by that same fence at another airport far away. I had dreamed those same dreams but had been too much in awe of the gods who dwelt there. I had never been able to be so daring and so bold as to cross the fence and approach the airplanes and those who flew them.

I climbed out and pushed the 172 backward into the hangar, which had a familiar musty smell of generations of birds, gasoline and oil. Listening to the cooling engine metal crack and ping, I almost heard the old airplane sigh. I wondered if it knew a little dream had been nourished that evening. Before leaving I stood beside it and remembered the hours we had spent together, the trips we had flown, the times we had shared happiness and fears. I thought of a wife and children needing food and clothes and shelter and education. I thought of taxes and Arabs and oil and of transponders and locator beacons and airworthiness directives and the ponderous FAA. And I thought of the teacher's salary that could no longer cover it all.

Then I pulled the little piece of newsprint from my pocket. I had it memorized. *For Sale, Sacrifice* . . . and it went on, describing the Cessna, ending with my telephone number and the advice to call after five o'clock. I was glad I was alone, for my eyes were moist.

In the next tale, Howard ''Pug'' Piper decided to chronicle fourteen close calls since he started to fly in the 1930s. Pug was vice-president of research and development and then executive vice-president of the aircraft company founded by his father, William T. Piper.

It took me some fourteen painful lessons to get it all down right. That works out to one every thousand flight hours over some forty-four years. Much of that time was accumulated when flying was more adventurous than it is now, and a fair portion involved test flights. Even so, it is not a good record.

The scorecard starts back in the 1930s. After a few hours of dual, I was flying around the Bradford, Pennsylvania, airport with my fiancée in a Cub. Our subsequently happy association was almost nipped in the bud when, during a turning approach, I slowed the Cub too much. It fell off into a half-turn spin and came out of it in a clearing, at an altitude about half as high as some nearby trees. From this, I learned *never* to let an airplane get too slow, particularly during the approach.

The next two incidents both resulted from the same misbehavior: buzzing. The first one is a bit hazy; all that comes to mind is a recollection of flying around Bradford in a Cub in the middle of a rain shower and buzzing the airport. All of a sudden, a roof appeared through the rain-smeared windshield, dead ahead. We missed that one . . . but not the next.

A few years later, flying a Piper J-4 from Bradford to Lock Haven on a clear summer morning, I decided to travel the last twenty miles down the Susquehanna River just above the water. I didn't think there would be any wires, since the area was undeveloped, but suddenly there were several loud pops, a flash, and the airplane jerked around a bit. Some individualist had strung an electric wire over the river, but I'd just put his lights out. My copilot, having read somewhere what to do in an emergency, reached up and turned the ignition off. The airplane still seemed to be flying, so I turned the ignition back on, and we proceeded to Lock Haven at a somewhat more respectable altitude. The prop was chewed up, and there were a few holes in the fuselage fabric where the wires had whipped around, but by the time the guy who owned the wires inquired, the airplane was as good as new. The moral, I finally learned, is simply to stay high enough so that you can't run into something.

In 1936, I was flying yet another Cub over Pennsylvania en route to Washington, D.C. Not far from Lock Haven, where the ridges grow to 1,700 feet above the valleys, the clouds above me started to gather around the tops of the ridges. Thinking they'd stay scattered, I climbed above them and proceeded toward Washington. Half an hour later, the cloud cover had gone from scattered to broken to undercast. I decided I'd better get on down, not knowing where I was or what was below. I finally broke out—well below the ridges and between a couple of them. The lesson was very simple and clear: no more flying on top in a VFR-only airplane.

We were doing quite a bit of barnstorming in the late 1930s, partly to publicize Piper airplanes and partly to bring in some badly needed dollars. We would take a couple of Cubs, find some town with a good-sized hayfield nearby, and start hauling the spectators at a dollar a head. I recall one small field with a haystack on which I snagged the tailwheel during a somewhat overloaded takeoff. Fortunately, the wheel just carried a wisp of hay along for the ride.

And that wasn't my only small-field scare: I had dropped off my wife-to-be in a tiny field with trees at both ends next to her college in Massachusetts. Helen had removed the rear control stick in the Cub for comfort, and after landing, she'd put it back on its stub. But she forgot the pin that secured it. On the following takeoff, which I made from the rear seat, I was startled to find the stick loose in my hand just after the airplane left the ground. I must have shoved it onto its stub rather hurriedly, for the field couldn't have been more than 800 feet long.

Nowadays, we don't have to worry about incidents like the last two. You just don't go around landing in any old field, and while this spoils some of the fun we used to have, it has its safety advantages.

Shortly before the war, a remarkable little wooden airplane was developed by Al Mooney—the Culver Cadet. It was one of the very few private planes with retractable landing gear. To prevent a gear-up landing, a pin moved in behind the throttle lever on the carburetor after the gear was raised, so it wasn't possible to throttle back for landing until the gear was down. Pretty clever.

But someone had overlooked the possibility of putting the gear down while practicing power-off stalls, then putting the gear back up again and pushing the gear-warning pin *in front* of the throttle arm. This is exactly what I did in the course of one flight, after which I unwittingly descended to about 50 feet for a speed run down the local railroad track. The immobility of the throttle led to a very hurried reextension of the gear, but it was too late.

So I landed in a field, at which point the gear came up. It turned out to be a good thing, because about 20 feet ahead of where the airplane had so precipitously stopped was a ditch that would have transformed the airplane and me into a pile of splinters. If there is a moral, it's to know your aircraft systems thoroughly.

Just before the war, a team of Piper pilots attempted to prove to the Army that Cubs could be useful as spotter and liaison planes. During one of the demonstrations, another pilot and I left our Cubs parked alongside the strip while we ate lunch. Suddenly, realizing that a thunderstorm was inbound, we ran over to secure the airplanes before the wind got to them, but arrived a minute too late. My airplane took off backward with me hanging onto the struts. This time we did end up in a ditch. Didn't damage much, but the lesson was obvious: always tie the darn things down if they're of a type that blows away easily.

Since World War II, I've had three serious engine problems, leading me to the conclusion that flying single-engine airplanes at night, in low IFR conditions or across oceans is for the birds.

Once, flying VFR right over an airport, I noticed oil suddenly coming through firewall openings and onto my feet. A gasket on the rear of the engine had failed, and in a very few minutes the engine would have seized.

During a flight in an early Aztec, a black streak of liquid showed up on the right nacelle. The engine was running smoothly, and there was no indication of trouble on the gauges, so we proceeded to our destination, thinking there was a minor oil leak. Actually, a fuel line had broken, and although it was still feeding the engine, it was also spraying gasoline all over the engine compartment. Coming out through the cowl webbing, it had picked up the black coloring.

The last engine incident also occurrred in an Aztec, this time en route to Europe. When I turned final for a landing at Gander, Newfoundland, the tower reported that the left engine was smoking badly. At the same time, we noticed that the landing gear wouldn't come down; hence a hasty conclusion that we had a broken hydraulic line and an engine fire—and what's more, that the gear wouldn't extend, because the emergency extension system doesn't work with a broken line. I considered a quick belly landing but decided to try hand extension of the gear during a hurried go-around. It worked, and the gear locked down. We landed with the fire trucks racing along behind and flames belching out of the left exhaust. Our problems were all the result of the failure of a drive gear that was part of both the hydraulic pump and the left turbocharger oil scavenging system. Had that little gear waited another hour or so to break, out over the Atlantic in a heavily loaded airplane, we could have had a problem. My wife had been complaining that these overseas flights weren't exciting. This time, she wasn't sure she wanted to get back into the airplane.

Two gear-up accidents in Comanches paid off handsomely, as it turned out. While checking the stall characteristics in an early Comanche, I turned off the gear warning horn, then forgot to turn it on again and scraped the belly of the airplane. During a takeoff in another Comanche, the gear somehow came up just after rotation. The airplane settled, prop knocking the ground, and my son, who was flying, put the Comanche down on its belly. Neither of us had moved the gear switch, so it must have been in the up position when we started the takeoff roll. These mishaps led to some effective improvements, most notably the almost foolproof landing gear on the Cherokee Arrow.

Finally, there was The Disaster. While making an instrument approach in conditions that were supposed to have the clouds above the ridges, my Twin Comanche ran into the top of a mountain at 1,750 feet. The altimeter was reading between 2,500 and 3,000 feet. It was one of those accidents that people never survive, but amazingly, my passengers and I weren't even badly hurt. Evidently, we hit the tops of some trees, then ran into heavier foliage and dissipated the airplane's energy over a distance of about 200 feet. It was like driving down a highway in the fog at 150 miles per hour and having the road suddenly end in a stand of trees. There was a flash of green, an incredible racket, and then we were sitting in what was left of an airplane in the middle of a clammy forest. This happened during a time when a number of altimeters were reported to be sticking. Whether that was what happened to us will never be known, but when one considers all the IFR approach accidents, it's obvious that a good case can be made for a backup altimeter.

Pug Piper admitted his mishaps for the same reason everyone else does in the ILAFFT column: he might encourage someone not to follow suit. And that added a bright side to some of his darker moments.

In the next and final confession in this collection, William F. Buckley, Jr., takes the lid off a succession of horrendous errors he made in the airplane he kept while at Yale. He tells the tale in the mood of carefree abandon that got him into trouble in the airplane all those years ago. It makes for amusing reading, and it will make every pilot cringe.

I had no fear of flying when I matriculated at Yale, but a very considerable fear of my father's learning that I had taken up a sport that, in 1946, he was unprepared to concede was anything more than rank technological presumption, fit only for daredevils. It turned out that several of my co-conspiritors had fathers with similar prejudices, so that when our little syndicate was formed, we all agreed that communications to each other on the subject of our surreptitious hobby would go forward discreetly, lest they be intercepted. During the Christmas holidays, it was my duty to send out the accrued bills from the little grass strip airport at Bethany, Connecticut, where we lodged *Alexander's Horse* (as we called the little Ercoupe), and I realized, envelope in hand, I could not remember whether T. Leroy Morgan, one of the six partners, was a junior. With a name like that, I felt he must surely be a junior—was there any other excuse? On the other hand, if I wrote "Jr." after his name and my friend was in fact the "III," then his father would open the letter. I assumed his father must be formidable, since who else would live at One Quincy Street, Chevy Chase, Maryland?

So, to play it safe, I addressed the envelope to: "T. Leroy Morgan—the one who goes to Yale, One Quincy Street, Chevy Chase, Maryland." It happened that, at the breakfast table distributing the mail among the family, Mr. Morgan *père* displayed an imperious curiosity about the contents of a letter so manifestly intended to be seen only by his son.

I will contract the suspension and say that in no time at all, word passed around a circle of fathers, reaching my own. Whenever my father was faced with a rank transgression by any of his ten children, he replied to it in one of two ways, sometimes both. His first line of attack would be to announce that the child could not afford whatever it was my father disapproved. He tried that for an entire year in his running war against cigarettes, but the effect was ruined when we all saw *The Grapes of Wrath* and Henry Fonda, between heaves of hunger, kept smoking. His second line of attack would be to ignore the delinquency, pretending it simply did not exist. Thus one of my brothers, who hated to practice the piano, was relieved from ever having to play it again by the simple expedient of being held up by my father in public discussions of the matter as the most exemplary pianist in the family.

I received a brisk memorandum (his reproachful communications were normally rendered in that mode) advising me that he had "learned" that I was "flying an airplane" at college, and that the distractions to my academic career quite apart, I clearly could not afford such an extravagance. One didn't argue with

Father, who in any case would never return to the subject except in a vague, sarcastic way. Three years later, he would write my prospective father-in-law, "You will find it very easy to entertain Billy when he visits you. You need only provide him with a horse, a yacht or an airplane."

And so for the few months of our joint venture, we continued to pass around the bills, like tablets in pre-Christian Rome. They were not, by current standards, frightening. Our capital was $1,800—$300 apiece. We paid exactly that for the secondhand airplane. We decided, after getting quotations from the insurance companies, to insure ourselves to a $300 deductible, payable by the offending partner. Anyone using the airplane would pay his own gas, oil and instructor. All capital improvements would have to be approved unanimously. Anybody could sell his one-sixth interest at any time. Reservations to use the airplane would be fixed with the secretary of the *Yale Daily News*. These, we satisfied ourselves, were surely the most informal articles of association in modern social history, though I suppose it is appropriate to add that the association was one of the briefest in history.

I was off to a very bad start. My experience was akin to arriving at a casino for the first time at age twenty and winning a dozen straight passes at the crap table. When Bob Kraut, my instructor—a dour, hungry, ex-Army pilot, ex-mechanic, owner of a starving little airport, who would sell you anything from a new airplane to a Milky Way—took me up for an hour's instruction, I could not believe how easy it all was. I remember it to this day: check the oil, check the gas, turn your wheel and check ailerons, pull and check elevator. Run your engine at 1,500 rpm, check one magneto, then the second, then back to both. Then gun her up to 2,250. Then exercise the knob that said "carburetor heat." Then head into the wind (or as close as possible at the single strip field), push the throttle all the way forward, roll down the strip, when you reach 60 miles per hour ease the wheel back, and after the plane lifts off, push the wheel forward to level until you reach 80 mph. Then adjust your trim tab to maintain a speed of 80 mph. Rise to 600 feet on your course, then turn left until you get to 800 feet. Then do anything you want.

Landing? Go back to approximately where you were when you hit 800 feet and proceed downwind twice the length of the field while descending to 600 feet. Then turn left descending to 400 feet. (I forgot something: you should pull out your carburetor heat when you begin your descent.) Then turn in toward the field, reducing your throttle to idling speed, coast down, glance sideways—which helps perspective—don't let your speed fall under 80 mph till you are over the field, then keep easing the wheel back until your tires touch down, at which point *immediately* set your nosewheel right down; Ercoupes, you see, had no separate rudders, the wheel incorporating that function—a nice advantage except that you cannot cope easily with crosswind landings.

The first lesson consumed an hour, the second a half hour, and that very night I was speaking to a forlorn junior who had been a pilot during the war and grieved greatly that he could not be the following day at dinner with his inamorata in Boston. Why could he not? Because his car wasn't working, and no train could get him up in time, since he could not leave until after lunch. I found myself saying, as though I were P. G. Wodehouse himself, "Why my dear friend, grieve no more. I shall fly you to Boston."

It was all very well for my friend who, with 2,000 hours' flying, navigated us expertly to Boston, landed the airplane and waved me a happy good-bye. I was left at Boston Airport, headed back to Bethany, never having soloed and having flown a total of three times.

Well, the only thing to do was to proceed. I remembered that the plane came equipped with a radio of sorts and that my friend had exchanged arcane observations and sentiments with the tower coming in, so as I sashayed to the end of the runway, I flipped the switch—and found myself tuned in to an episode of "Life Can Be Beautiful." I truly didn't know how to account for this, and I remember even thinking, fleetingly, that when the traffic was light, perhaps the tower entertained area traffic by wiring in to the controller's favorite program. This bizarre thought I managed to overcome, but it was too late to stop and fiddle with a radio I hadn't been instructed in the use of, so I went through my motions, looked about to see that I wasn't in anybody's way, and zoomed off.

I was flying not exactly contentedly that bright autumn day. I felt a little lonely, and a little apprehensive, though I did not know exactly why. I was past Providence, Rhode Island, when suddenly my heart began to ice up as I recognized that either I was quickly going blind or the sun was going down. I looked at my watch. We should have another hour and a half of light! Ah so, except that I had neglected to account for the switch overnight away from daylight saving time. I had put my watch dutifully forward at about midnight but today I thought in terms of light until about 7:00 P.M., same as yesterday. I looked at the air chart, so awfully cluttered and concentrated by comparison with those lovely, descriptive, onomatopoeic ocean charts you can read as easily as a comic book. I discerned that the New York, New Haven & Hartford railroad tracks passed within a few hundred yards of the airport at Groton. I descended, lower and lower, as the white began to fade, as from an overexposed negative soaking up developing solution. By the time I reached Groton, I was flying at 100 feet, and when I spotted the lights on the runway for the airfield, I was as grateful as if, coming up from the asphyxiative depths, I had reached oxygen.

I approached the field, did the ritual turns and landed without difficulty—my first exhilarating solo landing; my first night landing; on the whole, the culmination of my most egregious stupidity. But there we were: the plane and pilot, intact. I hitchhiked to the station, waited for a train, and by 10:00 P.M. was sitting at a bar in New Haven chatting with my roommate about this and that. I never gave a thought to Mr. Kraut.

I have been awakened by angry voices, but by none to equal Robert Kraut's the following morning. He spat out the story in volleys. While hauling the plane from the hangar, an assistant at the airfield had overheard me conversing excitedly with my friend on my impending solo flight from Boston to Connecticut. In the internalizing tradition of New England, he had said nothing to me about my projected violation of the law. But he spoke to his boss about it later in the afternoon, who exploded with rage and apprehension. Kraut called the tower at Boston, which told him of an Ercoupe having landed and then taken off at 4:07 P.M., without communication with the tower. Kraut calculated that I would arrive in the Bethany area in total darkness and thereupon began frantically collecting friends and passersby, who ringed the field with their headlights, providing a workmanlike illumination of a country strip. Then they waited. And waited. Finally, at about 10:00, Kraut knew I must be out of fuel and, therefore, on the ground somewhere other than at Bethany. Whether alive or dead, no one could say, but at least, Kraut growled into the telephone, he had the pleasure of *hoping* I was dead. *Why hadn't I called him*? I explained, lamely, that I did not know he even knew about my flight, let alone that he thought to provide for my safe return. He consoled himself by itemizing lasciviously all the extra charges he intended to put on my bill for his exertions and those of his friends, which charges the executive committee of *Alexander's Horse* Associates voted unanimously and without extensive discussion would be paid exclusively by me.

I got my clearance to solo; and, twenty flying hours later, my license to fly other people. I am compelled to admit that I cheated a little in logging those twenty hours, giving the odd half hour's flight the benefit of the doubt, listing it as one hour, and I feel bad about this. But I did achieve a limited proficiency, and I would often go out to the field and take up a friend for a jaunty half hour or so in my little silver monoplane, though I never felt confident enough to do any serious cross-country work, having no serviceable radio.

I remember two experiences before the final episode. In the early spring I invited aboard a classmate, a seasoned Navy veteran pilot. We roared off the lumpy field under an overcast that the mechanic on duty assured us was 1,200 feet high. It wasn't. The Bethany airport is 700 feet above sea level, and at 1,000 feet, we were entirely enveloped in cloud. I had never experienced such a thing and the sensation was terrifying, robbing you, in an instant, of all the relevant coordinates of normal life, including any sense of what is up and down. We would need, I calculated, to maintain altitude and fly south until we figured ourselves well over Long Island Sound. Then turn east and descend steadily, until we broke out unencumbered by the New England foothills; then crawl over to the New Haven Airport, which is at sea level. I willingly gave over the controls to my friend, Ray, who assumed them with great competence as we began our maneuver. Then suddenly there was a hole in the clouds, and he dove for it, swooping into the Bethany strip, landing not more than three minutes after our departure. I stayed scared after that one and resolved never again to risk flying in overcast.

Then there was the bright spring day with the lazy-summer temperature. My exams, it happened, were banked during the first two days of a ten-day exam period. In between I did not sleep but did take Benzedrine. Walking out of the final exam at 5:00 the second afternoon, numb with fatigue and elation, I was wild with liberty, and I knew I must stretch my limbs in the sky. So I drove out to Bethany, pulled out *Alexander's Horse* and zoomed off by myself, heading toward downtown New Haven and climbing to 4,000 invigorating feet. There I fell asleep.

I have ever since understood what they mean when they write about the titanic intellectual-muscular energy required to keep one's eyes open when they are set on closing. What happened was that the drug had suddenly worn off, and the biological imperative was asserting itself with vindictive adamance. It was, curiously, only after I landed that I found it relatively easy to summon the adrenaline to stay awake for long enough to make it back to my bedroom. In the tortured fifteen minutes in the air, my eyes closed a dozen times between the moment I discovered myself asleep and the moment I landed. It is safer to learn these things about the human body aboard a sailboat than an airplane. Boats can be dangerous, but they don't often sink when you go to sleep at the wheel.

My final flight, like so many of the others, was propelled by a certain mental fog. My best friend at Yale became engaged to my favorite sister. All my siblings had met Brent, save my poor sister Maureen, cloistered at the Ethel Walker School in Simsbury, Connecticut. I would instantly remedy that, and I wrote my sister, age fifteen, telling her to send me a map of the huge lawn that rolls out from the school (which I had many times seen while attending various graduations of older sisters). It arrived by return mail—on all accounts the most nonchalant map in the history of cartography. At the east end she had drawn vertical lines marked "trees." Running parallel from the top and bottom of that line to the west were two more lines, also marked "trees." At the extreme left end of the paper she had marked "main schoolhouse." Armed with that map and my future brother-in-law, I set out on a bright spring afternoon for Simsbury, which was about an hour's flight away.

I found the school and flew around it a couple of times with a creeping agitation. My sister having advised her classmates of my impending arrival, the entire school was out on the lawn, and, on spotting us, a greet cheer reached us through the roar of the little engine. The trees at the east side happened to be the tallest trees this side of the California redwoods. I buzzed them a time or two. Could they really be *that* tall? I estimated them at a couple of hundred feet. That meant I would have to come over them, then drop very sharply, because a normal landing approach would have had me three-quarters down the length of the lawn before touchdown. "Well," I said to my stoical friend, "what do you say?" Fortunately, he knew nothing about flying.

I was terribly proud of the way I executed it all, and I wished Mr. Kraut had been there to admire the deftness with which I managed to sink down after skimming the treetops, touching down on the lawn as though it were an eggshell. I looked triumphantly over to Brent as our speed reduced to 30 mph. The very next glimpse I had of him was, so to speak, upsidedownsideways. We hit a drainage ditch, unmarked by my carefree sister, that traversed the lawn. The problem now was quite straightforward. The aircraft was nosed down absolutely vertical into the ditch, into which we had perfect visibility. We were held by our seat belts, without which our heads would have been playing the role of our feet. We were there at least a full minute before the girls came. I am not sure I recall the conversation exactly, but it was on the order of:

"Are we alive?"

"I think so."

"What happened?"

"Ditch."

"Why did you run into it?"

"Very funny."

"Well, why didn't you fly over it?"

"We had landed. We were just braking down."

But the girls, with high good humor, giggles and exertion, managed to pry us out. We dusted ourselves off outside the vertical plane, attempted languidly to assert our dignity, and were greeted most politely by the headmistress, who said she had tea ready in anticipation of our arrival. We walked sedately up the lawn to her living room, accompanied by Maureen and two roommates. The talk was of spring, Yale, summer plans, the Atlee government and General MacArthur, but Maureen and her friends would, every now and then, emit uncontainable giggles, which we manfully ignored. It all went moderately well under the circumstances until the knock on the door. An assistant to the headmistress arrived, to ask whether her guests had any use for—

"this," and she held forth *Alexander's Horse*'s propeller or, rather, most of the propeller. I told her thank you very much, but broken propellers were not of any particular use to anyone, and she was free to discard it.

Eventually we left, having arranged by telephone with Mr. Kraut to come and fetch the corpse at his convenience. We returned to New Haven by bus. Brent, who had a good book along, did not seem terribly surprised, even after I assured him that most of my airplane rides out of Bethany were round trips.

Oh, the sadness of the ending. The plane was barely restored when, during a lesson, one of my partners was pleased by hearing his instructor say as they approached the strip for a landing, "You're hot!" My friend figured, in the idiom of the day, that this meant he was proceeding splendidly, so he nosed the ship on down, crashing it quite completely. As he later explained, what reason did he have to know that, in the jargon of the trade, to say you were "hot" meant, "You're going too fast"? He had a point. The estimate to repair *Alexander's Horse* was an uncanny $1,800—exactly what we had paid for it. Mournfully, we decided to let her rest, selling the carcass for $100. Father was right, as usual. I couldn't afford to fly.